CLASSIC WOODCUT ART

JOHN R. BIGGS

CLASSIC WOODCUT ART AND ENGRAVING

An International Collection and Practical Handbook

BLANDFORD PRESS
London · New York · Sydney

This edition first published in the UK 1988 by Blandford Press
Artillery House, Artillery Row, London SW1P 1RT

Copyright © 1958 Blandford Press Ltd,
and © 1988 Blandford Publishing Ltd.

Distributed in the United States by
Sterling Publishing Co. Inc.,
2 Park Avenue, New York, NY 10016

Distributed in Australia by
Capricorn Link (Australia) Pty Ltd
PO Box 665, Lane Cove, NSW 2066

British Library Cataloguing in Publication Data

Biggs, John R.
 Classic woodcut art and engraving : an
 international collection and practical
 handbook : wood engravings and linocuts
 by related methods or relief print making.
 — 2nd ed.
 1. Wood-engraving
 I. Title II. Biggs, John R. Woodcuts,
 wood-engravings, linocuts and prints by
 related methods of relief print making
 761'.2   NE1225

ISBN 0 7137 2021 2

Original typesetting in Monotype Bembo 12 on 14 point by the Dolphin Press,
Brighton.
Printed in Great Britain by Biddles Ltd, Guildford, Surrey.

CONTENTS

[2] VAN GELDER *Decoration*, Actual size (Dutch)

ILLUSTRATIONS
including diagrams

Frontispiece **FRANK MARTIN** *Bridge of San Luis Rey*
Engraving and cutting, printed from the wood

7

WOODCUTS AND WOOD-ENGRAVINGS

PREFACE

OOKS giving examples of woodcuts historical and contemporary are numerous; books describing how to make a wood engraving are many; books giving instruction in the craft of woodcutting are more rare; books attempting to describe in detail the tools, materials and methods of both woodcutting and engraving and at the same time including a wide range of examples of prints are, perhaps, rarer still. This book, we hope, will fall into the last category.

Can an art or craft be learned from a book? No book can transform anybody who has no artistic feeling into an artist; no book can make a craftsman of a person who has no bent; but anyone with reasonable aptitude may acquire the rudiments of a craft like wood engraving or woodcutting from books alone.

As evidence I can quote my own experience. I had a wood-engraving of mine hung in the Royal Academy (for what that is worth) before I had so much as met a wood engraver. The book which kindled my enthusiasm, which is undimmed after over a quarter of a century, was the pamphlet of only sixteen pages by Douglas Percy Bliss, 'Woodcuts, or the Practice of Engraving and Cutting upon Wood'. I cycled thirty miles into Leicester, which was the nearest town where gravers could be purchased, bought two tools and plunged (or is it lunged?) happily into the wood. I immediately discovered that wood engraving suited my temperament better than etching which I had been more or less forced to do at the art school I was attending.

Fortune provided fuel for my already growing interest when the doctor who took the place of the retiring family physician proved to be the brother of Douglas Percy Bliss. An attack of influenza brought him to my bedside and with him, a copy of his brother's new 'History of Wood Engraving'. This was shortly followed by a prize which took a form that combined an old interest in the theatre with the new interest in wood engraving, to wit, 'Woodcuts and Some Words', a most inspiring book by Gordon Craig. Since then wood engraving has provided me with a great deal of pleasure, a

9

creative outlet, and some financial reward. I should like to think that this book may do for others what D. P. Bliss's booklet did for me.

It is a pity that there is not a convenient term that covers, without being misleading, both wood-engraving and woodcutting. Xylography is already employed and the International Society of Wood Engravers is known as XYLON; but xylography is surely too pedantic for general use. Until such time as a better term is thought of we must be content with the ambiguous 'woodcut', in the sense defined in the Introduction.

There is also widespread inconsistency in the spelling of the words (or word) wood engraving. Should these be two separate words; should they be linked by a hyphen; or should it be one word only? By custom wood cut has become woodcut and wood cutter is now woodcutter. There has been a tendency for similar pairs of words to become one, and it is possible that wood engraving will eventually become woodengraving. I was inclined to assist evolution by printing woodengraving throughout this book, but so many friends were disturbed by the sight of the word woodengraving that I am led to bow to custom and make two words of it. There is, however, a possible difference of meaning between wood engraving and wood-engraving. We shall talk, therefore, of the process as wood engraving and the practioner as a wood engraver. But the print or block, the single entity, we shall refer to as a wood-engraving.

The illustrations, with the exception of the few historic examples, have mostly been produced in the '50s'. There is technical virtuosity, traditional restraint, experimental passion expresed in many individual idioms. Woodcut (and wood engraving) is no longer imprisoned in books — though the book is still one of the happiest settings for wood engravings — but is free to follow where the imagination of the artist-craftsman leads. Prints are tending to be bigger in size than ever before (as much as five feet by three feet) and can rival paintings as decorations for the walls of the smaller homes of today.

Because many of the original prints are large there is inevitably some loss in reduction to a size to fit this page. On the other hand, because the actual scale of line is important in the appreciation of prints we have made sure that many engravings are reproduced 'same size' and a number are printed direct from the wood. A great diversity of styles and techniques is represented and we trust that among them any aspiring engraver will find something to his taste, and on which he can base and fashion his own style.

INTRODUCTION

IN THIS BOOK the term WOODCUT is used to designate collectively woodcuts, wood-engravings, linocuts, and cuts or engravings on any material for printing in relief. Stencils are also included where these are used in association with the other three techniques. The term has long been so used in museums to classify relief prints printed from any material. It makes a considerable difference to the artist whether he works in wood, metal or linoleum, and though theoretically he should exploit the nature of the material, it is not always evident from the print what the printing block was made of.

Relief prints are made from blocks in which the white parts of the design are cut away as valleys below the surface, leaving the design as plateaux to receive the ink, which is transferred to paper by means of pressure. The blocks may be made of various woods or metals, linoleum, plastic, or even cardboard, and the tools may be knives and gouges or gravers. Different techniques are required to manipulate such a diversity of tools and materials and we shall describe the techniques of woodcutting, wood engraving, lino-cutting and stencil cutting. Each of these techniques by itself is capable of producing aesthetically satisfying results but today many artists are mixing techniques to create very exciting prints. The writing of this book is approached in the belief that a too purist attitude can be inhibiting, and that provided the aesthetic result is worth while, there is no reason why any or all available techniques should not be used on the same print. The aim is to create visual images by whatever means the artist's imagination suggests rather than to produce technical exercises within the limits set by preconceived and arbitrary rules. The end justifies the means.

But mixing of techniques cannot be done judiciously unless the unique qualities of each medium are appreciated. The first distinction to be made must be between woodcuts and wood-engravings. Each of these will be dealt with more fully in later pages; for the moment, it is sufficient to say that wood *cuts* are made with a knife and gouges on planks of softish woods in which the grain runs along the plank, and that woodengravings are made with gravers on the end grain of hardwoods, usually box (Fig. 4.).

WOODCUTTING This is by far the oldest of the techniques of making relief prints. The earliest known print from wood blocks is of two Buddhist charms, Wu-Kuo Ching-Kuang Ching, by order of the Empress Shotoku of Japan, A.D. 762–769. The earliest dated printed book (printed from wood blocks) is the Diamond Sutra of A.D. 868, in which there is a frontispiece depicting the Buddha discoursing to Subhuti, his aged disciple. It is a most accomplished and elaborate design, drawn in black line, containing over twenty human figures. There is reason to believe that in 868 (as also later in the great period of Japanese woodcuts, the 18th and 19th century) and in

[3] FIFTEENTH-CENTURY METAL CUT

Europe during the 15th and 16th centuries, an artist made the drawing and another craftsman cut the blocks.

Woodcuts began to be generally used in Europe at the beginning of the 15th century for the production of devotional prints and playing cards. All such prints are mainly in black line with practically no areas of solid black. They are, for the most part, crude in drawing and roughly cut, but many have great charm. Most were intended to be coloured by hand, the lines forming the boundaries of the different colours. Later in the century, in

WOOD ENGRAVING　　WOODCUTTING

Engraving tool

Knife

Boxwood
cut across
the grain
(end grain)

Pine, Pear
Cherry etc.
cut with
the grain.
(plank-
grain)

Sliver of wood removed by
one stroke of the graver.

At least two cuts needed to
remove a sliver of wood.

[4] *Wood engraving and woodcutting compared*

Florence, woodcuts of greater aesthetic interest were produced in which the black line was relieved by ingeniously placed areas of black—perhaps a window, a doorway, a dress or a book. These possess the boldness, directness and 'respect for the wood' which was lost as craftsmen became more techni-

[5] FIFTEENTH-CENTURY FLORENTINE CUT actual size

cally expert and were able to make facsimiles of an artist's pen drawing. This division of labour between artist and engraver (strictly a 'cutter') is to be seen at its best in the prints attributed to Dürer and Holbein. These are not creative woodcuts in the sense we wish to encourage in this book, but pen or brush drawings by very distinguished draughtsmen reproduced with astonishing virtuosity. The woodcut in the 15th and 16th centuries is used

[6] FRANK MARTIN *Bridge of San Luis Rey* The black is printed from the wood engraving, the colour from the woodcut

not so much as a medium having qualities and beauties in its own right but rather as a means of multiplying an artist's drawing.

With certain exceptions, the woodcut was used mainly as a means of reproduction until comparatively recent times.

The revolution in the arts which occurred in the 19th century, when traditional methods were challenged and a new vision was born, affected also the art of the woodcut. Many artists who were evolving new ways of making pictures and finding new ways of looking at things turned to the woodcut as a medium of artistic expression. Perhaps because the craft had been so long neglected they were able to take it up without being hampered by tradition. The public had fixed ideas of what they thought a painting should look like, but woodcuts, as distinct from 'trade' wood-engravings were unfamiliar. Gauguin and Edvard Munch (the great Norwegian artist who is now getting some of the credit he deserves) used the wood block in a way that had never been used before and produced prints of great originality and expressiveness. They proved that the making of prints is as worthy of the talents of a great artist as painting. Hitherto, woodcuts had been made apparently on the assumption that the printing would be done by a trade printer and therefore every tone had to be composed of carefully considered widths of line or stipples—every part of the printing area to be given the

Der Sternenseckher.

[7] HANS HOLBEIN *Dance of Death*
Woodcut, actual size (German)

same thickness of ink and to be evenly printed. Foolproof, in fact. But Gauguin made use of the grain of the wood which he scraped and scratched. He lowered the surface of the block in parts so that less ink would be picked up and less transferred to the paper in printing. He appreciated that a good print requires art not only in the conception of the design and in the cutting, engraving, or otherwise preparing a printing surface, but in the nature of the paper, the quality and quantity of the ink and in the control of the pressure. Thus effects are achieved which cannot be obtained in any other way, so that the woodcut becomes a medium of truly creative expression and

Passio Christi ab Alberto Durer Nu:
renbergensi effigiata cū varij generis carmi
nibus Fratris Benedicti Chelidonij
Musophili.

O mihi tantorum,iusto mihi causa dolorum
O crucis O mortis causa cruenta mihi.
O homo sat fuerit.tibi me semel ista tulisse.
O cessa culpis me cruciare nouis.
Cum priuilegio.

[8]   ALBRECHT DÜRER   *The Smaller Passion*   Cut, reduced (German)

not just a means of multiplying a design thought of in terms of some other
medium. Both Gauguin and Munch used the knife and gouge with such
vigour and dash that the trade engravers were aghast. As R. J. Beedham,
himself a first-class reproductive engraver, in his admirable little book on
the craft says, some of the earliest examples, with their masses of unrelieved
black, rather look as if they had been engraved with an axe.

But Munch's cuts are alive, and have given vicarious life to many woodcuts, linocuts, wood-engravings and other black and white graphic media
through the great influence his work has had right up to the present time.
What are the special qualities of a woodcut? Let it be understood from the

beginning that whatever qualities of any medium are admired and exploited by one generation of artists, it is likely that the next generation will discover others. So that when attention is now drawn to certain characteristics and effects, it is not in any way intended that these should be thought of as final, but rather as a starting-off point for every craftsman to discover effects and qualities of his own.

By far the largest number of woodcuts in the past have been mainly in black line and this has led some people to think that woodcut is essentially a black-line medium. This is far from the truth. As we have already said, many of the early cuts were intended to be coloured by hand so that the woodcut, then, was more in the nature of a 'key' or guide to the colourist than an end in itself. Moreover, apart from the playing cards and devotional prints, most woodcuts were intended to be printed with type and the black line harmonised admirably with a page of type. Artistic fashion and the need to harmonise with type were therefore the prime reasons for the black line rather than the nature of the medium. In recent times there has been considerable interest in the opposite extreme—that of making the picture almost solid black with only a few areas of plain white paper and white lines. This can be very effective, particularly if the white shapes are interesting enough in themselves to stand up to the violent contrast with dense impenetrable black.

But there is no necessity to make areas solid black. The pattern of the grain of the wood can be incorporated into the design—in fact the piece of wood can be selected for the beauty of the grain or any pictorial possibilities it may suggest.

On the other hand, the beauties of the black line have been neglected lately, possibly because of the disparagement implied where writers and teachers say that because a black line is achieved by cutting away the background to leave the line standing, it is less 'artistic' than the 'direct' white line. Even so sagacious a critic, so imaginative an artist and so skilful an engraver as Douglas Percy Bliss said 'Wood-engraving is a freer, more spontaneous and more truly creative method' than woodcutting. One writer on wood-engraving went so far as to say ' "White line" alone is art'. This seems to show a lack of understanding of the nature of 'black line' in woodcut and wood engraving. Because the cutter (or engraver) must cut each side of a line separately and deliberately he is able to 'draw' each of the two contours of the line with conscious care. Each side of the line can be fashioned to give the maximum of effect. This gives the well conceived woodcut its characteristic line. Because the knife tends to cut in short straight lines, there is a tendency for the resulting black line to be composed of a series of facets, often barely perceptible, but giving a slightly chunky or angular line that is so different from a line made with a brush or pen.

In recent times, perhaps the greatest examples of black-line cuts are the illustrations by Maillol for 'The Eclogues of Virgil' and 'Daphnis and Chloe'.

[9]   ARISTIDE MAILLOL
L'Art d'Aimer
Cut (French)

White line in woodcut too has this delightful angular quality which is so different from the fluid, suave white line that is so easily achieved in wood engraving.

A *method* is neither creative nor uncreative. It is the artist's mind which creates and what the artist produces will be creative only if he is a creative artist. If he is not a creative artist what he produces will not be creative, whatever medium he uses, whether it is wood engraving, woodcut, water colour or oil painting. There is a world of difference between the old 'formschneider' patiently cutting away the background of a drawing done on the block by Dürer or Hans Baldung Grien, and a twentieth-century artist cutting his own designs, creating as he goes. With the knife or gouge in his hand the artist thinks in terms of his tools and materials and is not a reproducer of his own drawings any more than a painter in oils is a reproducer of his studies made in pencil, pen and wash, or water colour. The sketch is a guide for a creation in oil-paint made with brushes or palette knife. Similarly a sketch for a woodcut is a guide for a creation made with knife and gouge on wood.

Thought of anew, and forgetting that in the past most woodcuts were reproductive, woodcutting is as free and creative as wood engraving. Indeed, as far as freedom is concerned the evidence is that much freer, looser, more painterlike forms have been produced in woodcut than in woodengraving. Some of the colour prints produced in America since the Second World War, notably by Seong Moy and Adja Junkers, come very near to painting in the way the shapes have been organised and the colour handled, so that one is never conscious of the medium impeding the artist's invention. There is, however, no suggestion of straining the technique to produce effects more natural to oil paint. On the contrary, all the effects are inherent in the medium, and the beauty is that of a print in its own right.

There is no *one* 'natural' or 'right' way of designing for woodcutting or wood engraving. Maillol may use the black line, Munch may use large areas of solid black, Gauguin may have areas scratched and scraped, Wadsworth may create patterns of almost equal areas of black and white, other artists may have many white lines and again others may have many black lines in association with solid blacks and pure whites. The aim may be to create abstract forms or to represent nature as faithfully as the medium and the skill of the artist will allow. In between these two extremes, no matter what the artist's aesthetic creed, whether conscious or unconscious, the woodcut can be the adequate vehicle of the artist's imagination.

At the risk of making invidious distinctions here are the names of some artists whose work in woodcut or linocut may profitably be studied: Seong Moy, Adja Junkers, Antonio Frasconi of America; Edward Bawden, Frank Martin, Michael Rothenstein of Britain; C. K. Beck, Werner Berg, Slavi Soucek of Austria; J. J. de Grave of Belgium; Toini Kiviharu, Erkki Talari and Viotto Vikainen of Finland; Hap Grieshaber of Germany; M. Domjan of Hungary; Maxim Sedej and others of Yugoslavia; Walter Binder, Oscar Dalvit and Otto Tschumi of Switzerland; August Cernigoj of Trieste.

WOOD ENGRAVING The technique of engraving on the end grain of hard wood was developed towards the end of the 18th century. It is probable that blocks had been engraved on the end of the grain very much earlier, but it was Bewick who used the end grain of boxwood so successfully that it was to become the chief method of making relief prints during the whole of the 19th century. He was apprenticed to an engraver on metal and was therefore trained to use the graver, not the knife. What was more natural, when blocks were required by printers, than that he should continue to use the tool with which he was familiar, and to use the end grain of boxwood that enabled him to do so? But Bewick became himself a creative artist (which most 19th century wood engravers were not) and when he came to engrave his own work he was able to engrave creatively and was not under any obligation to make a facsimile of an artist's drawing as later engravers were expected to do. He thus drew directly with the graver in what we now call 'white line'. He had a superb sense of line and tone and texture, and his placing of accents of pure white and solid black is so absolutely right that it amounts to genius. But Bewick's reputation depends not only on his prodigious technical skill but also on his observation of nature, his sense of humour and his power as a creator of vignettes that caught the spirit of a landscape and a rural society in the space of two or three square inches. Bewick lives as a creative artist rather than as a technician, though like many great artists he was also a technical innovator.

Contemporary with Bewick were two other important artists whose work in engraving is influential today for its imaginative approach. They are Calvert and Blake. The total output of engravings by both artists was only a handful of blocks which, nevertheless, have earned for them a high reputation in the history of engraving and a position, not to be despised, in the history of British Art as a whole, even if they had produced nothing else.

[10] THOMAS BEWICK *Tailpiece* Engraving, actual size

[11] EDWARD CALVERT *The Return Home* Engraving, actual size

Calvert's blocks are exquisite gems of minute engraving brought to life with
poetic passion. To change the metaphor—they are little lyrics of black and
white illustration.

Blake, of course, was a poet in every sense. His poetic vision suffused whatever he did and the few wood blocks he engraved for Thornton's Virgil
display his unique power as an artist by evoking an atmosphere of poetry
and other-worldliness within the limited space of about four square inches.
Technically they are not outstanding; indeed, on publication, the publisher
apologised for them and allowed the printer to cut off about a third of the
already small area of the blocks. A heinous act of vandalism we still lament!
But even this mutilation could not destroy Blake's vision. One of the reasons
why Blake appeals to the mid-twentieth-century artist is that his passion was
so great that he was prepared to sacrifice technical proficiency to intensity
of expression. He proved that meticulous craftsmanship (however desirable
in theory) was not the most important quality in art. The best artists in the
20th century have more in common with Blake than with artists much
nearer to them in time.

The 19th century saw the rise of the commercial reproductive engraver
and again saw the division of labour we had seen in making woodcuts in the
15th and 16th centuries. Artists made drawings, or drew on the blocks (and
finally drawings were photographed onto blocks) for the engraver to inter-
pret or cut in facsimile. Engravers became more and more skilful at copying
artists' work, but themselves, became progressively less sensitive to artistic
qualities and, in the end, their work was as dead and depressing as it was
technically astonishing.

But let us be fair. Some of these reproductive engravers were sensitive
interpreters, the most famous being Swain, Linton and the Dalziel brothers.

[12] WILLIAM BLAKE *Thornton's Virgil* Engraving, actual size

The latter, in spite of Rossetti's gibe,* produced blocks better in many ways than could be produced today by line block or halftone. Who would replace by line blocks the engravings of Swain and Dalziel from illustrations by John Millais, Frederick Sandys or Boyd Houghton, or the Evans brothers' colour engravings of Kate Greenaway's designs?

But we are concerned here not with wood engraving as a means of reproduction but as a creative art and towards the end of the century, with the Arts and Crafts movement, came a recognition of wood engraving as a medium of original expression. Charles Ricketts and Charles Shannon and Lucien Pissarro were among those artists who strove to bring new life to the craft. The first two derived, perhaps, too much inspiration from 15th century Italy, but Pissarro had something original to say with the woodcut. But outside the stream of sophisticated art, Joseph Crawhall was producing books (quartos) with woodcuts in the chap-book manner that were full of vitality and one suspects that a number of successful engravers between 1918 and 1938 owed something to good old Joe. 'Olde Ffriends wyth Newe Faces' and 'Olde Tayles Newlye Relayted' are a perpetual delight. Sir William Nicholson followed with his 'London Types' and 'An Alphabet', which, though the bold open treatment makes one think of wood *cuts*, were in fact engraved on the end grain.

It was in between the two world wars that white-line engraving became so popular, and many fine engravers appeared who used the medium creatively and with individuality. A few names are: Eric Gill, Eric Ravilious,

---

*Oh woodman spare that block
Oh gash not any-how,
It took ten days by clock
I'd fain protect it now.
Chorus: Wild laughter from Dalziel's workshop.

Blair Hughes-Stanton, Gertrude Hermes, Vladimir Favorsky, Felix Vallotton, Dimitrov Galanis, Imre Reiner. Some are still, happily, practising. The illustrations in this book are evidence of the vigour with which woodcutting, linocutting and wood-engraving are being practised today, and though to mention a few names is to be exposed to the criticism of omitting other names that might be considered just as worthy, the work of the following will repay study: Misch Kohn, Lynd Ward, Leonard Baskin and Eugene Mecikalski in America; Vladimir Favorsky, Andrey Goncharov, Alexis Kravchenko in U.S.S.R.; Derrick Harris, Gertrude Hermes, Roderick Barrett, Cecil Keeling in Britain; Tranquillo Marangoni and Pietro Sanchini in Italy; Zbinden and Buchser in Switzerland; Pam Reuter, Thijs Mauve J. B. Sleper in Holland; Bruno Bobak and Lawrence Hyde in Canada; Hans Orlowski in Germany.

[13] JOHN R. BIGGS *Converting logs into planks* Engraving on the end grain of pear wood. Printed from the wood

WOODCUTTING AND LINOCUTTING

WOODCUTTING

THE WOOD   Woodcuts are made on wood which has been cut from the trunk as shown in the diagram on page 13, so that the grain runs along the surface and is referred to as 'plank grain'. The Japanese preferred cherry wood, but apple, pear and sycamore are used. Whatever the wood, if the proposed design includes fine black lines, and if all areas and lines are required to print evenly, an even regular grain is to be preferred. But artists working in the contemporary idiom are not inclined to be so purist. Many artists like to make use of the interesting patterns in the grain of the wood— a piece of wood with an attractive grain may even provide the initial inspiration for a print. This being so, it is unnecessary to employ the traditionally prescribed fruit-tree woods. Literally any kind of wood may serve the artist's purpose, but pine has much to recommend it. It is easily obtainable, it often has an attractive grain. It is, however, apt to be knotty, though knots may occasionally be incorporated into the design. Wood from orange boxes and other packing cases can provide serviceable blocks. Many plywoods have an interesting grain and are good so long as the top layer of the ply is thick enough to allow a clean line to be cut. Plywoods that are $\frac{3}{8}''$ thick and more have the advantage of not readily warping. If the proposed design is intended to be printed with type, the block should be type height ($\cdot918''$). But if individual prints are being made by burnishing or other means, there is no need for the wood to be much thicker than the depth required to be cleared in the largest area of white. Large areas of white require a greater depth than small areas. In colour prints, one kind of wood may be used for one colour and another kind of wood for another colour in the same print, so that the best use is made of the character and direction of the grain. The grain may run vertically in one colour and horizontally in another.

It is not always essential to plane the wood (whether obtained from the timber merchant or the grocer) because the texture printed by the rough sawn surface is sometimes fascinating. Textures obtained in this way must be carefully incorporated into the design of the print and not be purely fortuitous or accidental. Coarse woods such as those used in packing cases are only useful for bold, broad effects. It is rarely possible to cut fine black lines in such woods. Crude woods lend themselves to simple shapes with interest of surface; finer woods lend themselves to subtler drawing but less interest of surface in the print. The ease with which a fine black line can be cut depends partly on its direction in relation to the grain.

Variety and interest of surface texture in a print may be obtained by treating the surface of the wood in different ways. For example, a rasp may be used to roughen the area required to print with a broken texture; or a sculptor's claw may be hammered into the surface in a number of different directions. The knife may be used to make a number of criss-cross lines.

Acid may be used to emphasise the grain. This is done by rolling the block lightly with ink and then putting a few drops of dilute nitric acid to the areas where the grain is required to be emphasised. After a few minutes (varying according to the strength of the acid and the degree of emphasis desired) the block should be washed to remove all trace of the acid.

Anything that will roughen or lower parts of the block is potentially of value in producing textures, but it must be remembered that if the hollows made (with whatever tool) are shallow, they are likely to fill in easily and therefore only small editions can be printed from such blocks. On the other hand, if the incisions are reasonably deep, long editions would be possible.

As to size, the limit is set more by the size of good paper available and by the means of printing than by the wood. Planks of wood can be obtained from most timber merchants one inch thick and one foot wide (or wider if specially cut). These can be joined by the tongue-and-groove method described on page 43. The length can be up to ten or twelve feet, but this is impractical for printing. The largest single woodcut known to the author is about 72" long. The print by Hap Grieshaber on page 119 is 58½"by 21¾".

If blocks are to be printed on an orthodox printing machine which is constructed to take blocks the height of type, it is not only necessary that the wood should be type height but that it should not be warped. Warping can

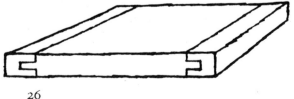

[14] *Block mounted with end pieces to prevent warping*

[15]   *Printed from untreated oak*

[16]   *Printed from untreated deal*

[17]   *Printed from apple wood. The cuts on the left were made with a knife; those on the right (top)
were made with a V tool; those on the right (bottom) with a gouge*

[18]   *Printed from plain deal. The tones are made by means of overlays (see page 70) on the cylinder
of the printing press*

[19]   *Linoleum. The texture on the right was made by rocking a gouge from side to side on its cutting edge. The lines and textures on the left were made with a V tool*

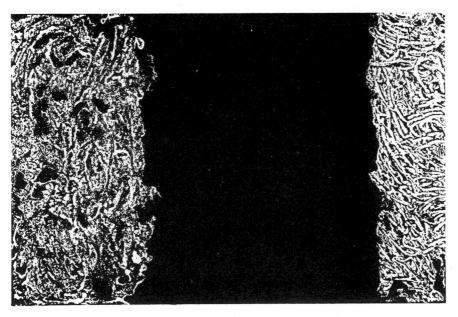

[20]   *Linoleum. Treated with alabastine (Reproduced by line block)*

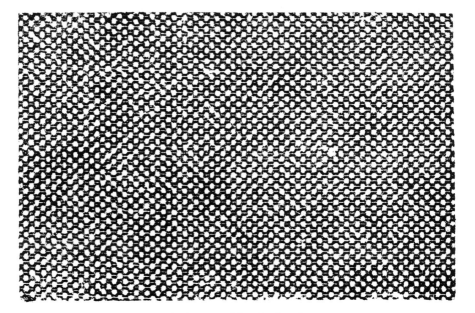

[21]   *Printed from hardboard*

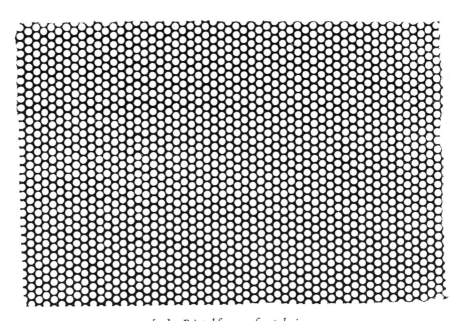

[22]   *Printed from perforated zinc*

be minimised by fixing a strip of wood across each end of the plank as in Fig. 14. The pieces of wood at each end have the grain running at right angles to the plank.

Slight warping is no serious detriment to a block which is to be printed by burnishing.

THE TOOLS

Tools for making woodcuts are few and simple, a knife and gouge being all that are strictly necessary. A few sizes of gouge and a few chisels make work easier and quicker though not invariably better. Descriptions of tools and equipment follow.

[23] *English-type cutting knife*

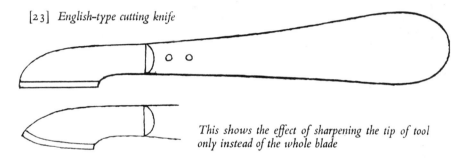

This shows the effect of sharpening the tip of tool only instead of the whole blade

THE KNIFE   This is the most important tool and with it all the parts of the design requiring precise drawing are done. There are two chief kinds of knife, the European, illustrated on this page, and the Japanese (Fig. 24). The

[24] *Japanese-type cutting knife*

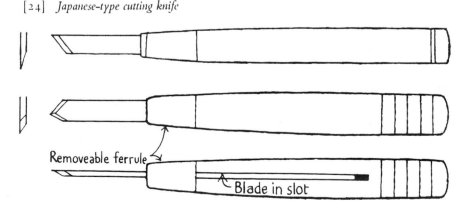

Removeable ferrule

Blade in slot

European knife is held in much the same way as we hold a pen or pencil. The flat side of the blade should be against the line being cut, and cuts are made by pulling the knife downwards towards the body. Considerable freedom of movement (and hence freedom of drawing) is possible with the knife held in this way; provided, of course, the grain is suitable. In contrast to

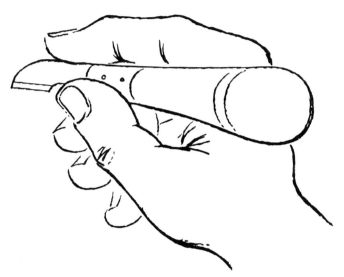

[25] *Method of holding the English knife*

engraving, in which lines can be engraved in all directions with equal facility, in woodcutting it is obvious that lines can be cut more readily along the grain than across it. Indeed, care has to be taken lest the knife runs unbidden along a ridge of the grain when cutting in the same direction as the lines of the grain. When cutting across the grain there is more resistance to the knife in the darker coloured lines than in the lighter coloured, pulpier parts in between. Hence there is the danger of a jerky cut and possible slips.

It will be seen from the diagram that the cutting edge of the European knife is about an inch long, though only about a quarter of an inch of it at the tip actually cuts the wood. The knife should be kept sharp on the India or Washita stone, and it is wiser to sharpen the whole length of the cutting edge otherwise, if the tip only is sharpened, it will gradually become curved.

There are two varieties of the Japanese knife: that in which the cutting edge is a single bevel at about 40 degrees across the blade, and the other in which there are two cutting edges which meet, as in Fig. 24. The latter is useful for 'facsimile' cutting in the Japanese manner but is not generally favoured by cutters who create as they cut. The normal Japanese manner of use is to hold the knife as one might a dagger, guiding the point with the thumb or finger of the left hand.

Some knives have a detachable blade which lies along a groove in the handle and is held in position by the tapered ferule which can be removed if the blade needs pulling up (Fig. 24.)

A practicable tool is a sturdy penknife, either with the blade shortened,

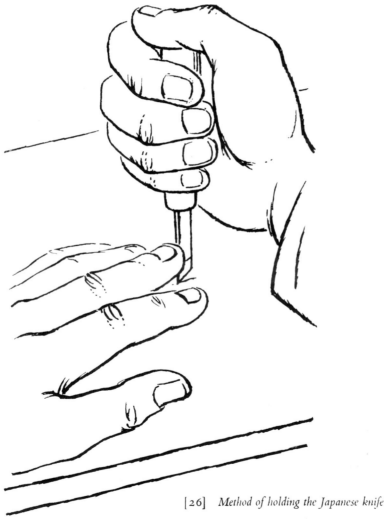

[26] *Method of holding the Japanese knife*

or bound with tape or cord and covered with rubber tubing, to make it comfortable to hold and to prevent it suddenly folding up. This is a very convenient tool for lino-cutting.

Whatever the tool, it should be kept sharp. A blunt tool is uncontrollable.
THE SCRIVE OR V TOOL   As the name implies, a V tool, is a v-shaped tool which will cut a channel in wood with one stroke only (a knife would take at least two strokes). They are obtainable in a variety of sizes as shown on the diagram on page 35 and are very useful for cutting a series of fairly uniform lines, or textures, and also for clearing corners. Within limits it is possible to 'draw' with the scrive, and it is tempting, because of the apparent saving of labour, to use it when the knife would give a more characterful line. Nevertheless, two or three sizes of scrive are desirable, and *one* is virtually indispensable. The scrive can be bought in a long handle as used by wood carvers or with a short blade inserted into a mushroom handle like an engraving tool. The latter can be manipulated with almost the ease and facility of a graver and should be held in the same way; any difficulty will be due to the nature of the wood, which varies in its cutting qualities from plank to plank and in different parts of the same plank.

It is less easy to 'draw' with the long-handled scrive, which is generally held in the left hand and pushed with the palm of the right hand or tapped with a mallet.
THE GOUGE   This tool is essential. It is mainly used for clearing spaces and it is advisable to have a number of different sizes. As will be seen in Fig. 27, a gouge is a curved chisel and the curve may vary from a small U to almost flat. Some are bevelled, and sharpened on the inside of the curve, others are bevelled and sharpened on the outside. Those sharpened on the inside of the curve are more accurate for 'drawing', but those sharpened on the outside are better suited to clearing spaces as they are less likely to 'bury themsleves' in the wood. Experience teaches one to judge which tool is best for a particular occasion.

Make sure when clearing spaces with a gouge that the boundaries are well and deeply cut with a knife, particularly across the grain, otherwise there is a likelihood of the gouge running along the grain and splitting off a larger piece than was intended. Different parts of the same piece of wood can vary very considerably in hardness, so always be on the alert.
THE CHISEL   The chisel is useful in a number of sizes, which range from about one-eighth of an inch to one and a half inches wide. The wide chisels

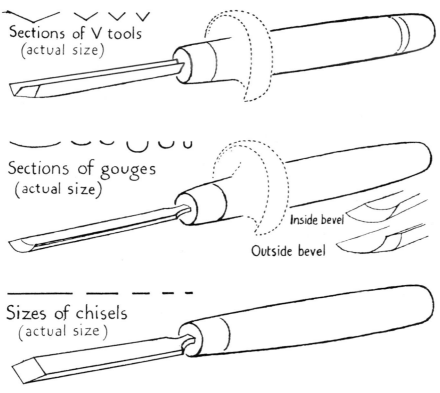

Sections of V tools
(actual size)

Sections of gouges
(actual size)

Inside bevel

Outside bevel

Sizes of chisels
(actual size)

[27] *Cutting tools: V tools, gouges, chisels*

are for cutting register marks and clearing large spaces where the gouge may have left ridges which pick up ink and thereafter print as unwanted marks. Small chisels are convenient for clearing corners in small spaces.

THE MALLET A small carpenter's mallet is frequently necessary to drive the chisel or gouge when clearing spaces. One with a head about two and a half inches across is big enough. A leather-headed mallet is kinder to the handles of chisels and gouges than a wooden mallet, and is better for controlling the cut.

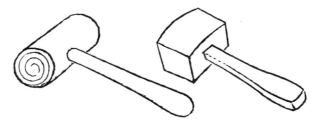

[28] *Mallets. The one on the left is leather-headed*

NUMBER AND SELECTION OF TOOLS The first essential is, of course, the knife. One, the European variety, is recommended, and for the professional craftsman a Japanese type as well. A small V tool or scrive is invaluable and two other sizes as shown on page 54 are a great help. Three chisels, one about an eighth of an inch wide, one about a quarter of an inch and one an inch wide are sufficient for most artists. A minimum of three gouges is desirable, a small U, a medium-sized U, and a flattish one will enable a wide range of work to be done, but more sizes will often save unnecessary labour.

CARE OF TOOLS The two best ways of storing the gouges, scrives, etc., are the cloth hold-all type and the specially constructed box with a place for each tool. The details given on page 54 need not be repeated: the only difference will be in size, to accommodate any long-handled tools. Chisels and knives are sharpened by holding the bevelled face of the tool flat against the oilstone and rubbing to and fro. The flat side of the blade should not be sharpened.

Gouges with the bevel on the inside of the curve require a slip-stone (Fig. 29) which is rubbed up and down with a little oil inside the curve, moving the stone from side to side to avoid wearing grooves in the bevel. Two sizes of slip-stone (either India or Washita) will sharpen a variety of tools.

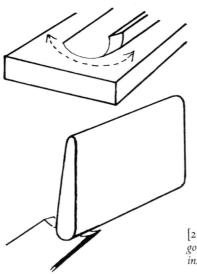

Remember to have one slip-stone with its smallest curve small enough to sharpen the smallest gouge. If the bevel is on the outside of the curve it can be sharpened on an ordinary flat oil-stone. The bevel is placed against the stone and the tool rotated backwards and forwards on its axis so that the bevel is rubbed at a constant angle. Facets on the bevel should be avoided.

[29] *Method of sharpening an outside bevel gouge on an oil-stone; and (below) sharpening an inside bevel gouge with a slip-stone*

BRUSHES   Because woodcuts are often printed with water inks, brushes are used to apply the ink instead of rollers. These may be of the type used by the Japanese (Fig. 30) or they may be ordinary house-painters' brushes, which are quite as good, for inking large areas. Small areas can be inked with the brushes either of sable or hog-hair used by artists for oil-painting. Small shoe brushes can be used for blending backgrounds, and old shaving brushes after retirement can have a new career creating effects on woodblocks.

[30]   *On the left, a Japanese brush; on the right an ordinary hog-hair brush*

CRAMP OR VISE   Because of the greater resistance offered by the wood in wood-cutting, whether with a knife, scrive or gouge, it is often advisable to hold the piece of wood to the desk by means of a cramp (Fig. 31). Cramps can be bought in many sizes, but the appropriate size will be governed by the thickness of the edge of your desk or work bench. The jaws of the cramp should be slightly larger than the thickness of the bench, plus an inch, an inch being the greatest thickness of wood likely to be used for wood cutting.

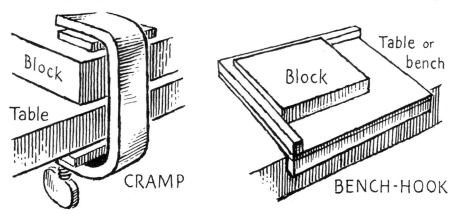

[31]   *On the left a cramp for holding block; on the right, a bench-hook*

BENCH HOOK   An alternative (or addition) to a cramp is a bench hook. This is simply a wooden tray having two raised edges on the top to prevent the wood being cut from slipping, and a projection on the underside to hold the whole to the edge of the bench. A bench hook can easily be made by

screwing two pieces of 1″ by 1″ batten along two edges of a piece of ⅛′ plywood, and another piece of batten on the under edge of the open side of the
tray thus formed. The diagram (Fig. 31) will make this quite clear.

LINOCUTTING

THE LINOLEUM The linoleum used for lino-cuts is ordinary furnishing
linoleum, preferably of the best quality, about three-sixteenths of an inch
thick. Though plain linoleum is made in a variety of colours, the most serviceable is the familiar brown. It is sold in rolls six feet wide at any large
furnishing store, where it is often possible to buy 'off cuts', that is, odd-sized
pieces left over from laying lino in a particular room. Grey 'battleship' linoleum about a quarter of an inch thick is favoured by some artists, but there
do not seem enough advantages in this grey lino over the usual brown to
justify the higher cost. Lino can be bought mounted (by gluing) on to wood
to the height of type. It is also available mounted on compressed cardboard
(type high) and is sold under the trade name of Baskertype. There is no
danger of this working loose from the mount, and Baskertype is therefore
particularly good if the block is to be printed (perhaps at the same time as
type) by a commercial printer.

THE TOOLS

All the tools used for woodcutting can be used to make linocuts, and all
that was said about tools on page 32 *et seq.* applies to linocutting. Lino being
a softer material than wood, a surprising freedom of line can be obtained
with a scrive. Inexpensive sets of tools for linocutting can be obtained with
easily removeable blades or nibs. These blades can be bought separate from
the handles and, when blunt, can be replaced cheaply. One V tool with cutting edges at about 45 degrees will make a wide range of thickness of line
and a variety of textures. This, together with a couple of gouges and a penknife, are enough tools to make very elaborate prints. Small useful gouges
can be made out of a length of old umbrella rib stuck in a cork.

Variety of surface texture in the print can be obtained in many ways.
Light inking and light pressure will allow the granular texture of the lino
to print. The surface of the lino can be scraped and scratched. The coarse
sanded paper sold by pet shops for use in the bottom of bird-cages will produce an interesting texture if laid, sand-side down, on the lino and passed
through the press. The grains of sand make pits in the lino which print as

tiny white dots. Another effect can be obtained by smearing a layer of glue and alabastine onto the surface. This can be stroked with a brush before it dries to leave the minute ridges of the brush strokes. When dry the alabastine is very hard and prints as Fig. 20. These effects are particularly well used by Michael Rothenstein, to whom I am indebted for this tip.

[32]   WALTER EGLIN   *The Drinker*   Cut, 19¼ by 16¼ inches (Swiss)

[33] REMO WOLF *Clowns Innamorati* Cut, 13¾ by 10 inches (Italian)

WOOD ENGRAVING

HE WOOD Engraving requires a hard, close-grained wood cut in slices across the trunk of the tree, as shown in the diagram on page 13. Holly, pear and other hard woods can be used, but none is so satisfactory as boxwood.*

Boxwood is obtained from trees related to the box, which is frequently seen as a low hedge at the side of garden paths. Box in England rarely grows to a size big enough to supply blocks for engraving in large enough quantities to be commercially practical. Indeed, the largest trunk of English-grown box the author has seen was only three or four inches in diameter.

The best wood is said to be Turkey box, but Mr. T. N. Lawrence, the chief manufacturer of engravers blocks in England, who has been in the business all his life, says that 'Turkey' box before the War (1939) was imported from Russia; today his best box (still often referred to as 'Turkey') comes from South Africa. John Jackson, the famous engraver, writing in 1838, says, 'American and Turkey box is the largest; but all large wood of this kind is generally of inferior quality, and most liable to split. . . . From my own experience, English box is superior to all others; for, though small, it is generally so clear and firm in the grain that it never crumbles under the graver.'

Papillon, an 18th-century French engraver, said he considered the large Turkey box inferior to that of Provence, Italy or Spain.

The quality of the wood varies in different parts of the same 'disc'. Those parts which are of an even yellowish colour are generally the best. Reddish parts near the heart are often tough or spongey and do not engrave well. When the annular rings are wide apart the wood is soft and not good for engraving very fine lines, but is quite satisfactory for bold open work.

When the logs (usually about 8″ to 12″ in diameter) arrive in this country

---

*It seems that the term box covers a variety of woods having similar characteristics. The best wood available in England, imported from South Africa (Cape box), is the *Buxus Macowanni*. But much of the boxwood used today is Maracaibo box from the West Indies and Venezuela (*Gossypiospermum Praecox* or *Casearia Praecox*).

they contain a large quantity of moisture and the wood must be seasoned for many years before it is in a suitable condition for engraving on. The logs are first cut into a series of slices (rounds) about 1″ thick. They are then stacked; each round overlapping the other, like bricks in a wall, and left to season by allowing cool, dry air to circulate round the wood for at least three years (Fig. 34). Many of the logs split, the cracks radiating from the heart of

[34] *How boxwood is stored for seasoning*

the trunk. The blocks for engraving obtainable from each round of wood are therefore not very large in size. It is very rare to see a single piece of box as big as 8in by 6in.

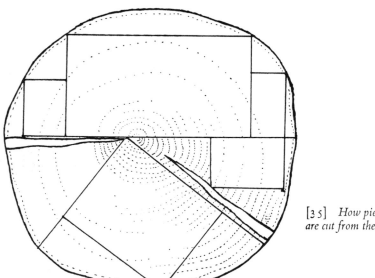

[35] *How pieces of boxwood are cut from the 'rounds'*

Large blocks are made by gluing a number of smaller blocks side by side. In France nothing but glue is used to hold the pieces together. In England the joints are made more efficient by a tongue and groove. That is, a groove about ⅜″ deep is cut by means of a circular saw into the edges of the blocks to be joined. A strip (tongue) of wood, usually mahogany, cut plankwise, of the same thickness as the groove and slightly less wide than the combined depths of two grooves, is inserted into the grooves together with thin glue, thinly applied (Fig. 36). The resulting joint is imperceptible to the touch when finished, and, unless the block is allowed to get damp or too hot by being left in the sun or too near a radiator, it is not likely to open during its normal working life.

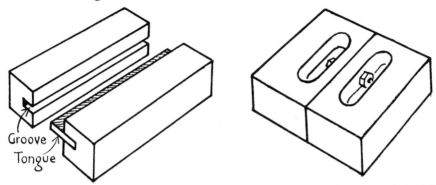

Groove

Tongue

[36] *How the pieces of wood are joined together; left, by tongue and groove; right, by bolts*

To prepare the wood for engraving, one surface of the block is planed smooth with an ordinary jack plane and smoothing plane, followed by a scraper. The final miraculous and exquisite smoothness is obtained by means of glass paper ('flour' grade). The block is then placed, finished side down, into a planing machine which reduces the thickness of the block to the height of type ($\cdot$918″, or the height of a shilling on its edge).

The keen engraver may like to try preparing a block for himself, but he is likely to find the time spent is very great and the result not nearly as good as the blocks supplied by the professional block maker.

The largest single woodengraving in the author's experience is a supplement to the 'Graphic' of 1884. It is a balloon's eye view of London from above the Houses of Parliament and is 33″ by 43½″. In those days blocks were joined by means of nuts and bolts as in the diagram on this page. The whole block was joined together and the drawing made on the surface (or sometimes transferred by means of photography). The block was then taken apart and each piece engraved simultaneously by a different engraver before being finally reassembled. In England today 18″ by 12″ would be thought of as a large block, but in America Misch Kohn has engraved blocks approximately 20″ by 30″.

Blocks should be stored away from damp or heat. Some people recommend storing them on edge rather than flat. The author has blocks in his possession which have been lying flat in shallow drawers (a printer's block cabinet) for twenty-five years without sign of deterioration. A good way of storing is to put each block in an envelope marked with the subject of the engraving and placed on edge in a bookcase packed reasonably tightly with books. But the bookcase should not be near the fire or near a window if the sun is likely to fall on the blocks.

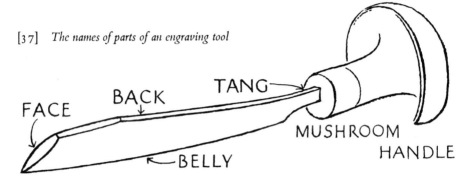

[37]   *The names of parts of an engraving tool*

THE TOOLS

The tools used in engraving are illustrated on pages 46 & 47. The length should be such that when the tool is in the working position as shown on page 53, the point is just beyond the tip of the thumb. If it is much longer it is difficult to control. A tool a little too short is better than one a little too long. It is best if the belly of the tool is slightly curved, but unfortunately most tools obtainable today are straight. They are usually too long as manufactured, but most suppliers will shorten the tool to suit each individual purchaser by cutting off the tang, that is, the part which is inserted into the handle. The tool may be shortened by the engraver himself in the following way. The tool is removed from the handle and a groove made in the tang with a triangular file or hacksaw at the point where the break is to be made. It is then put into a vise with the groove slightly above the jaws of the vise and given a smart blow with a hammer. The surplus piece of tang should then snap off at the filed groove. The tool should then be tapped carefully back into the handle.

[38]   *Shortening the tang*

The angle of the face to the belly should, generally speaking, be about 45°. If the angle is too obtuse the graver will not only engrave less easily but the shaving will tend to curl over on itself, thus hiding the line about to be engraved (Fig. 39). On the other hand, if the angle is too acute, though the

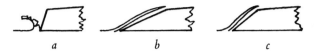

[39]   *Angle of face:* (a) *too steep,* (b) *too shallow,* (c) *about right*

shaving will glide smoothly over the face, the point is liable to break off; particularly if the tool is accidentally tilted at too great an angle so that the point buries itself in the block.

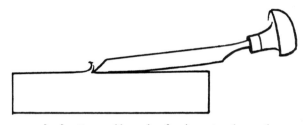

[40]   *Reasonable angle of tool entering the wood*

Some manufacturers number the sizes of their tools, but these vary so greatly from maker to maker that a number is not an accurate guide to the size of a tool. It is better to visit the shop and select tools by sight and, preferably, by trial on a piece of wood. If tools are ordered by post, the actual size of the cross sections should be given, together with the length measured from the point to the base of the handle.

There are three kinds of engraving tool: (1) those primarily used for engraving single lines of variable width: gravers, spitsticks and bull stickers; (2) those for engraving lines of even width; tint tools, multiple tools, and fine scorpers; (3) those for clearing spaces: round scorpers, square scorpers, chisels and gouges. All tools can also be used to make stipples. All tools are made in many different sizes. All tools can be bought without handles and inserted into whatever kind of handle the engraver prefers. Some engravers favour a piece of cork, but the kind illustrated is the most popular.

[41] GRAVER OR BURIN *Showing the section of three actual sizes, and an engraved block demonstrating the cuts made with this tool*

[42] SPITSTICK *Note the curved sides to the face of this tool which is most versatile and particularly well suited to the cutting of curves*

[43] ROUND SCORPER *Mainly used for clearing out spaces, but the smaller sizes can be used for enlarging outlines. Makes good stipples*

THE GRAVER OR BURIN This is the oldest and simplest of engraving tools and differs from the metal engraver's burin only in the angle of the face with the belly, the metal engraver needing a more obtuse angle (Fig. 39). It may be square in cross-section, or lozenge shaped; both kinds being available in many sizes (Fig. 41). It will engrave lines of varying width by altering the depth of the point. The deeper the graver is driven into the wood, the wider the line. Theoretically, then, a line of any width from the finest scratch to the maximum width of the tool is possible. In practice this is not so. A fine line engraved with a large tool (say a square graver) is likely to be too shallow and therefore readily fills up with ink in printing. A wide line made with

46

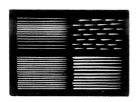

[44] TINT TOOL *Suitable chiefly for making parallel lines of even width, but is good for outlining straight objects. Does not make curves well*

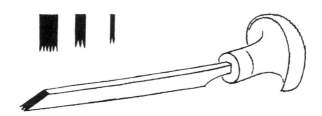

[45] MULTIPLE TOOL *This tool can produce interesting textures some of which can be seen in the block on the left. Apt to be 'flashy'*

[46] SQUARE SCORPER OR CHISEL *Used for clearing spaces, making textures, and beveling the edges of blocks. The texture on the bottom left is made by rocking the tool to and fro as it moves along*

small tool would be uncontrollable; even, perhaps, impossible to make, owing to the resistance of the wood if the point goes too far below the surface. Also, if the lines were close together, the black line separating them (remember every engraved line is a white one) is likely to have too little supporting bevel and thus be in danger of breaking down under the pressure of printing. The diagram Fig. 61 makes this clear. What is here said of the effect of the depth at which the graver is worked applies also to the tint tool, spit stick and bull sticker. It is evident, then, that every size of tool will only engrave a limited number of widths of line efficiently. That is, every tool has its 'natural' width of line. While it is possible to make a complete picture with

47

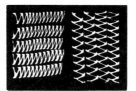 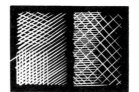 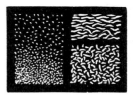

[47]   *Here and on opposite page are tones and textures made with*

one tool only, the range of width of lines is bound to be restricted, although in the hands of a good artist the result may be aesthetically superior to an engraving made with the greatest armoury of tools.

The burin *will* engrave a series of lines of equal width, but this is not easy, because the slightest variation of pressure will alter the width of line very noticeably.

As the tool enters the wood the line engraved will start at zero width, but as the tool goes deeper into the wood the line will get wider and wider. If the tool is then maintained at an even depth the line will be of constant width. If the tool is lifted abruptly, the line will end bluntly. On the other hand, if the point of the tool is brought gradually to the surface the line will taper back to zero (Fig. 48). Short stabs with the graver give an interesting stipple of tiny triangles. Longer stabs produce long, tapering triangles.

Curved lines can be engraved with a burin but there is a tendency for the edges of the lines to be bruised.

THE SPITSTICK   Without doubt, this is the most versatile of all engraving tools. It is not mentioned in the famous 'Treatise on Wood Engraving' by Chatto and Jackson in 1838, which contains one of the most comprehensive and thorough descriptions of the *craft* of wood engraving we know. Even in the manual of instruction in Woodengraving (1884) by W. J. Linton, himself one of the best trade woodengravers of his day, this tool is not mentioned by name. Nevertheless he says, 'A very slightly rounded tool, allowing of some limited variety of line, yet not tending to so much divergence as the graver, was always a favourite tool with me for soft and delicate and nicely graded shades.' His diagram makes it clear that what he meant was a spitstick, but it is also clear that such a tool was not generally used and was not

[48]   *Burin gradually pressed deeper into the wood and gradually raised.*

Lines re-entered   Swelled lines made with one stroke

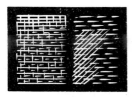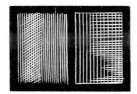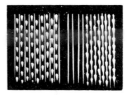

various tools. On the extreme left a square scorper was rocked to and fro

so named. R. John Beedham, also a trade engraver, writing in 1921, speaks of the spitstick by name and ranks it higher than the graver in usefulness. Many writers since then have referred to this tool as a spitsticker. The addition of the 'er' does not appear to be an improvement.

The spitstick cuts curved lines more sweetly than any other engraving tool. As with the burin, increased pressure rapidly increases the width of the line. Lines of uniform width may be cut by maintaining even pressure. Short stabs produce a stipple composed of dumpier triangles than those yielded by the graver. It is the best tool for the beginner to practise with and when competence has been achieved it is likely to be the most frequently used tool.

THE BULL-STICKER   This is virtually a spitstick with bulging sides. The line it makes will therefore have a very rapid 'spread'. It is particularly useful for making stipples and for clearing corners by thrusting it down into the block at about 45°. Care should be taken not to dig too deeply, otherwise the point is liable to be broken.

THE TINT TOOL   To nineteenth-century reproductive engravers (and to the few remaining trade engravers today) this was a most important tool because, as the name implies, it was devised to cut 'tints' or shades of even tone. But such mechanical accuracy is little valued by many contemporary artist-engravers and is less used than the burin and spitstick. In fact, some artists would discourage its use because of the natural tendency to produce lines of mechanical evenness. The tool has flat sides, and the section is a very narrow isosceles triangle. It is evident that with a tool of this section, increases in depth of cut will only very slightly increase the width of line. The slight variations in depth, almost inevitable when making a number of parallel lines, are virtually imperceptible in the lines produced.

It follows from what has been said that wherever a series of regular straight lines of uniform width is required the tint tool is best. Some of the best English artist-engravers employ areas of flat grey in their designs and therefore find the tint tool invaluable. The tint tool will not engrave curves well.

It is useful for outlining areas having straight contours—for example, the straight strokes in lettering, buildings, windows, furniture and the like. It is easier to make a *straight* line with a tint tool than any other. Once a line is started, the belly of the tool lies along the incised groove and unless sideways pressure is exerted, the tool will tend to continue in one direction; hence the ease with which straight lines are cut by means of a tint tool. A tint tool will produce efficiently a line of one width only. Lines of different width are best made with different tools rather than by trying to vary the depth of the incision.

THE MULTIPLE TOOL   An invention of the reproductive engraver which enabled him to cover areas with lines of uniform thickness more quickly than with a tint tool, is called a multiple tool. It will engrave up to six, or even ten lines, with one stroke. (Eventually a machine was devised for this deadly task.) The multiple tool is difficult to maintain at an even depth for long strokes; in consequence, contemporary artist-engravers rarely use the tool. When they do, they usually use it in short stabs to create textures rather than to cover areas with lines of mathematical regularity. Nevertheless, the tool is not to be despised, and if handled with taste can yield interesting and worthwhile effects.

Rocking the tool from side to side as it is pushed forward gives the effect shown in Fig. 45.

A two line (white line) engraver will obviously leave a black line of even width between the two white lines. The space can then be cleared on each side. Therefore the tool can be used for 'drawing' where a black line of even width is intended.

One of the best ways of learning the discreet use of this tool (and for that matter the right use of any tool or technical device) is in the study of the work of the best artist-practitioners, some of which can be seen in this book and in the books mentioned in the Bibliography.

[49]   *Here and on opposite page are more textures*

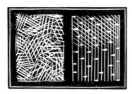  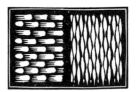

THE SCORPER   Jackson called this tool a 'scooper' and Beedham a 'scau-per'. Whether round or square, the scorper is mainly employed in clearing white spaces. The round scorper is by far the most useful. A fine scorper can be used to broaden a fine outline before clearing spaces, or it can be used for direct drawing of bold forms and lines. It is well suited to making bold brick-like textures and stipples of approximately semi-circular dots (Fig.43).

The larger scorpers are used for clearing large spaces.

Square scorpers are handy for taking out corners but care should be taken not to undercut the finished work. The wider square scorpers of, three-sixteenths or a quarter of an inch, are virtually chisels and are very useful for clearing away space round the edge of the block. Lines on the edge of the block are liable to break away; it is therefore sound practice to make a slight bevel with the

[50]   *Square scorper bevelling edge of block*

square scorper before engraving such lines. Rocked to and fro as it is pushed forward, the square scorper produces the texture shown in Fig. 49.

BRUSH   An old toothbrush or other small brush is useful for removing fine shavings that are apt to choke some of the engraved lines.

NUMBER AND SELECTION OF TOOLS   It has already been said that it is possible to create a satisfactory engraving with one tool only, but there is no virtue in producing an effect with difficulty with one tool when another tool will produce the same effect much more easily and quickly. On the other hand, a large range of tools will not necessarily result in better work. Different craftsmen have their own favourite tools and would perhaps give a different selection from the one given here which is, nevertheless, one based on over a quarter of a century's experience as a practitioner and, later, as a teacher of engraving.

The beginner is advised to start with three tools only—a fairly fine spit-stick, a medium spitstick, and a medium scorper. As the 'feel' of the tools is developed—and it is to be presumed that appreciation of the aesthetic qualities of the medium will develop at the same time—more tools may be

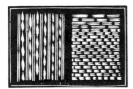

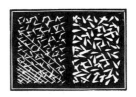

added. It is probable that the first additions to the range of tools will be scorpers. In most designs there are spaces which are too small to clear with a large scorper but which would be tedious to clear with a graver or spit-stick and which would most likely leave fine ridges just below the surface which would 'foul' in printing. Three round scorpers is a workmanlike selection. One of them should be fine for running round outlines, and one of them fairly large to speed up the clearing of large white spaces. A three-sixteenths of an inch square scorper is also desirable.

The taste in design or style of the artist is likely to influence the choice of additional tools. If the artist's taste is for bold shapes and simple textures, he might be happy with one spit stick and one scorper. If he enjoys the sensu-ous quality of textures and relishes the actual handling and manipulation of the tools (for there is great physical pleasure as the tool glides silkily across the wood like a skater on ice), he is likely to want one or two more sizes of

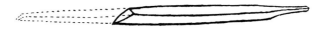

[51]   *Old file, shortened and ground to make an engraving tool*

spitstick, graver, and tint tool. He may also like to try one or more multiple gravers which can increase the range of effects obtainable. Love of the materials and delight in the handling of the tools is essential to success in any medium, but it should not be at the expense of artistic expression or creative vitality. The tools and materials should be servants not masters. But servants, to give of their best, need understanding and should be given the treatment their nature requires.

An excellent tool can be made from an old file. A triangular file with about quarter inch faces is convenient for the purpose. The file must first be heated (a silversmith's 'hearth' and blow-lamp are ideal) until it is cherry red, and allowed to cool. This softens the metal, otherwise it would be extremely difficult to cut and shape. With a hack-saw cut off the file to the required length. Remove the ridges of the old file from the two faces which will form the belly of the tool. This is best done on a grindstone, which will also grind the angle of the face of the graver-to-be. During this operation care must be taken to avoid overheating of the point, otherwise it will become too brittle. If a spitstick is required, the belly can be ground to the desired

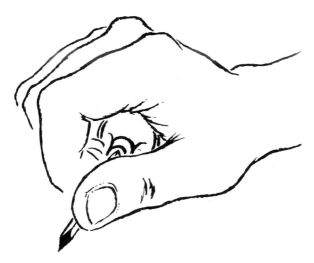

[52] *Top view of how the graver should be held in the hand*

size and section. A file can be used to shape the tool if a grindstone is not available. The marks of grindstone or file can be removed on an oilstone. When this is done the steel must be hardened again by heating until the glowing metal reaches a pale straw colour at the cutting edge, when it must be instantly 'quenched' by plunging the tool into a vessel of cool oil.

With the addition of a handle, and after sharpening the point on an oilstone, the tool should be ready for use. Two of the author's favourite tools were made in this way.

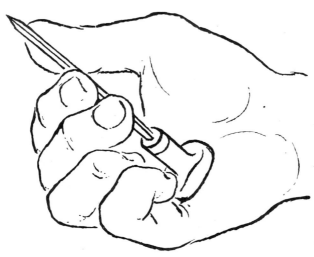

[53] *Underneath view of hand holding graver. Note that the point of the tool is just beyond the tip of the thumb*

53

CARE OF TOOLS All tools of all crafts should be treated with great respect and not least the tools for engraving. First, they must be properly housed or stored. The necessary condition for storage is that the point and cutting edge of the belly should be preserved from damage. The two most efficient ways of keeping engraving tools are illustrated on this page and page 55. One is a 'hold-all' of felt, baize, or similar material. Down the middle is sewn a strip of petersham about one and a half inches wide. It is attached to the baize or felt at intervals, leaving loops just sufficient to take the bellies of the tools. The flaps are folded over the tools and then rolled and tied with tapes attached to one end.

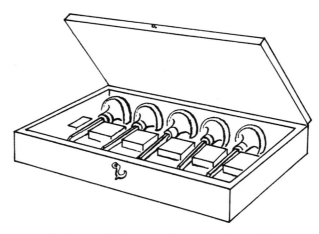

[54] *Box for keeping tools. A cigar box will do*

The other method is to make a box, or use an empty cigar-box, in the bottom of which are glued pieces of wood at intervals, leaving gaps just wide enough to accommodate the bellies of the tools. The bottom of the box is better if lined with felt or baize. Less space will be needed if the tools are laid alternately point to handle as in the diagram of the hold-all.

It is obvious that steel tools should never be allowed to get damp otherwise they will rust. If the tools are not being used for any length of time, a wipe with an oily rag over the face and belly will prevent rust.

Most important is to keep tools really sharp.

THE SANDBAG The purpose of the sandbag is to support the block while being engraved. It is comprised of two circular pieces of leather sewn together at the edges and stuffed tightly with fine sand before the last few

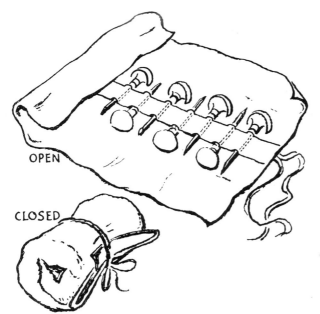

OPEN

CLOSED

[55] *Hold-all of baize which is excellent for keeping and carrying engraving tools*

stitches are made. Any other strong material which will hold sand will do instead of leather—but it is hardly worth the trouble of making a sandbag oneself—it is best to buy one. The advantage of a sandbag is that it enables the block to be tilted slightly during engraving. The size should be six or eight inches across. Smaller ones are not convenient for engraving large blocks, whereas a large sandbag is appropriate for both small and large blocks. If economy must be considered, a sandbag might be dispensed with altogether and the block supported on a pile of old magazines, or books of a convenient size and thickness, wrapped in brown paper.

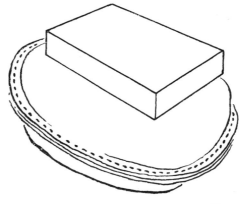

[56] *Sand-bag with block in position ready for engraving*

55

OILSTONES   These are most important and should always be at the engraver's side when he is engraving. It is best to have a hard Arkansas stone, which need not be larger than 1 inch by 2 inches, for keeping a keen edge on tools. From time to time the stone should be wiped and, if necessary, cleaned with fine sand, otherwise it will become clogged with oil and too slippery to be effective. If a tool has become very blunt or the tip broken, a coarser,

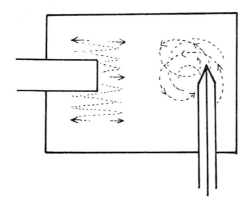

[57]   *Sharpening tools. Square scorpers and chisels are sharpened with a straight to and fro movement; gravers, spitsticks, etc., are rubbed on the oil-stone with a circular motion.*

more cutting stone should be used before finishing off with an Arkansas. A fine carborundum or an India stone is appropriate. A practical and inexpensive general purpose stone is a Washita. These coarser stones might reasonably be six inches by two inches in size as they are useful for sharpening other tools as well as gravers and wood-cutting knives.

Thin oil should be used with both kinds of stone.

THE MAGNIFYING GLASS   It is best to engrave with the unaided eye and avoid the use of a magnifying glass, whether of the watchmaker's monocle type or of the large reading-glass type. Why engrave lines which will need a magnifying glass for them to be appreciated? Moreover, when a lens of any sort is being used, only a portion of the block is visible, which makes it more difficult to perceive the true relationship between the part being

[58]   *Piece of card used as a fulcrum under the scorper when clearing spaces. The card prevents the printing surface from being bruised*

engraved and the rest of the design. If, however, a particularly fine or delicate passage must be engraved, for example a tiny face or hand or small lettering, a lens can be helpful. This is virtually a reading glass fixed to a supporting stand with means to adjust it to the right height and to the correct angle in relation to the block.

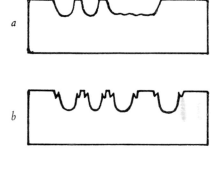

[59] *Sections of blocks showing*

(a) *Correct cutting and clearing of space. Note good clean bevel.*

(b) *Avoid the shoulder just below the printing surface which is likely to print. This should be cleared to give a bevel as in (a)*

(c) *Bad undercutting of printing surface. The overhanging parts are liable to break off.*

THE GLOBE   This is a glass globe, rather like a goldfish bowl on a stand, filled with water and placed between the block and the lamp when the engraver is working at night. Its purpose is to concentrate the light on the part of the block being engraved and to protect the engraver's head from the heat of the lamp. This was very necessary in the days of oil lamps. Nowadays a globe—even if it can be said to justify the extra space it takes up on the engraver's desk—is a luxury.

[60] *Spaces are best cleared by taking off a succession of smaller pieces as in* (a) *rather than as in* (b)

a

b

[61] *Depth and width of engraved line*
(a) *too wide and shallow*
(b) *too narrow and deep*
(c) *about right*

a

b

c

PREPARING THE BLOCK FOR ENGRAVING

The boxwood comes from the maker with an astonishingly glossy surface which is much too slippery to draw upon with a pencil. Reproductive engravers of the last century reduced the gloss and gave sufficient 'bite' to the surface by rubbing with finely powdered bath-brick or a mixture of bath-brick and flake white. This method may still be employed. A slightly damp rag is dipped in a saucer of bath-brick and rubbed gently over the surface of the block until the extremely high gloss is removed. When the surface is quite dry again it may be stroked once or twice with the palm of the hand to remove any surplus bath-brick. One should then be able to drawn on it quite clearly with a pencil or brush. Lines drawn with too soft a pencil tend to rub out too easily; a hard pencil or a pen may bruise or scratch the wood; a brush is considered by many artists to be best.

Another method is to brush the surface with a thin film of Chinese White, but the object is the same, namely to produce a dark drawing on a light ground. This was no doubt best for the old reproductive engravers who were interpreting other artists' work. But today the artist-engraver trains himself to think more in terms of the tools and this in turn leads him to favour a blackened, not a whitened, block for engraving. Every stroke made on a blackened block immediately appears as a positive white line, and the block, as the engraving proceeds, has virtually the appearance of a print. This fosters direct creative, white-line work.

The best way of darkening the surface is by applying ordinary blue-black writing ink. This stains the surface a pleasant cool black that contrasts beautifully with the creamy-white lines of the wood exposed by the graver. The ink may be applied to the block with a brush, a bit of rag or paper, or the finger with equal efficiency. Streaks should be avoided. The more even the tone of the surface ink, the easier it is to judge the engraved tones as work proceeds.

Fixed, or waterproof Indian ink, is not satisfactory because it dries on the surface as a thin film which peels or flakes off. Unfixed Indian ink, or the black writing inks such as Waterman's Jet Black or Swan 'Old English' Manuscript Ink, will do, but in the writer's opinion blue-black writing ink is best.

TRACING THE DRAWING It is hardly necessary to state that the bold and confident engraver may sketch the main lines of his design direct on the block. But most people need to prepare a sketch and to trace the essentials

58

on to the block. It is most convenient if the sketch is the same size as the intended engraving.

It is best to have a piece of tracing paper either large enough to be folded neatly under the block—like wrapping a parcel—so that it will not move during tracing; or just large enough to fold about half-way down the sides of the block where it can be fixed with sellotape or other adhesive. The main lines of the design should be traced from the sketch with a fairly soft pencil and with moderate pressure to make sure enough of the lead of the pencil adheres to the tracing paper. The tracing may then be placed, *pencil side down*, on the block. The thin very transparent tracing papers allow the drawing to be visible even on the blackened block, but sometimes it is necessary to lay the tracing, pencil side down, onto white paper and lightly indicate the lines on the back so that they are visible when laid on the blackened block. The lines should then be traced with a hard, sharp pencil pressing sufficiently hard to transfer some of the lead from the tracing paper to the block but not so hard as to bruise the wood. A steel tracing point may be used but an H or 2H pencil is adequate. It is advisable to lift one corner only of the tracing at first so that if, after inspecting the tracing, some lines are too faint, the paper can be replaced in exactly the same position and the faulty lines re-traced. The pencil line on the black surface, at best is rather faint, but is usually enough for the engraver to see. If it is too faint it may be desirable to go over the lines with a finely pointed HB pencil. All this means going over the same lines many times; but at each stage the aim should be to improve the drawing. Tracing should not be thought of as a mechanical operation but rather as an opportunity to make a better drawing, using the original drawing visible through the tracing paper as a guide.

Another method is to use yellow or white carbon paper. A tracing from the sketch must be made, and the carbon paper placed between the block and the tracing paper. It is then traced with a hard pencil or tracing point. It is important to remember to turn the tracing over, otherwise the engraving will print the reverse (from left to right) of the original drawing. An advantage which the first method described has over the use of carbon paper is that it is practically impossible to forget to reverse the drawing.

Whether the design is sketched directly on the block, or whether it is traced with pencil or carbon paper during the course of the engraving, the drawing is liable to be rubbed away. Some artists recommend spraying the surface with 'Fixative' (Shellac dissolved in spirit) which will prevent the drawing being rubbed away. Fixative is sold by all dealers in artists' materials. It is used primarily for fixing pastel, charcoal and pencil drawings, and is applied by blowing through a tube as in Fig. 60.

Whether the drawing is fixed or not, it is wise first to engrave lightly the main lines of the design—it then does not matter if some of the detail gets blurred. In fact, it can be something of an advantage because the mind must be kept constantly alert and creative—not lulled into reproducing a drawing done in another medium.

If a design is extremely complicated and intricate so that the engraver shrinks from the tedium of tracing or fears serious loss in accuracy, it is possible to have the design reproduced on the block by means of photography. The surface of the block is coated with a light-sensitive solution; a negative is made of the design which is placed against the surface of the block and exposed to light long enough for the dark areas of the design to appear sufficiently dark on the block. It is possible for the artist to prepare and apply a light-sensitive emulsion himself—but it is scarcely worth the trouble. Far better to employ a professional photographer, and if your local photographer is not able to do this, T. N. Lawrence, who supplies the wood blocks, will arrange to have your design photographed onto the block.

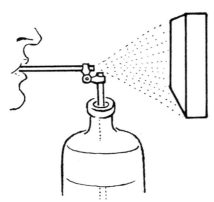

[62] *Drawing on surface of block being fixed by spraying with Fixative*

LOWERING   Blocks do not always print exactly as the engraver intended. Where fine lines or delicate tones emerge into areas of white there is a tendency for those lines and tones to print too heavily. The pressure can be adjusted by means of 'make-ready' (see page 70), but fine lines normally receive just as thick a film of ink as do the solids. Nineteenth-century engravers discovered that by making the surface of the block slightly lower where light tones were intended, greater delicacy could be obtained. The process is known as lowering and is carried out by means of a chisel tool or a scraper of the type that etchers use (Fig. 63). Lowering must be done before lines are engraved; therefore, when the main lines have been traced, the light

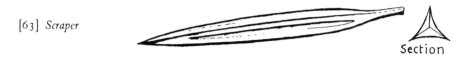

[63] *Scraper*

Section

tones should be carefully scraped to the required depth, which should only be a little below the surface, otherwise no ink at all will be picked up from the rollers. It is obvious that the hollow should be quite smooth. The lowered part may then be blackened again and the tracing replaced and those parts of the design retraced. The block is then ready to be engraved. It is essential that the tools used for engraving lowered areas should have slightly curved bellies.

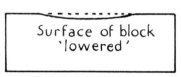

Surface of block 'lowered'

[64]   *Section of 'lowered' block*

[65]   *Clearing corners by directing the tool downwards*

Some piecemeal lowering may be done as work proceeds, for example, where a few black lines are surrounded by large white areas the lines can be scraped or shaved with a chisel tool even after engraving.

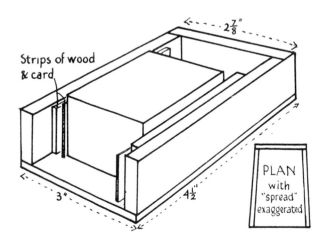

Strips of wood & card

$2\frac{7}{8}''$

[66]   *Small 'galley' for containing little blocks, thus being more convenient to hold while engraving*

$3''$

$4\frac{1}{2}''$

PLAN with "spread" exaggerated

[67] VLADIMIR FAVORSKI *Title page* Engraving, actual size (Russian)

PRINTING

ASIC PRINCIPLES and methods of printing and the equipment required for printing woodcuts, wood-engravings and linocuts are the same.

The simplest method of obtaining a print is by burnishing the back of the paper to be printed while it is in contact with the inked block. The only equipment required is a burnisher and a piece of thin card to place between the burnisher and the paper.

BURNISHING Burnishing has one advantage over printing in a press—the pressure can be controlled in great detail. Some parts can be rubbed lightly so that only a thin greyish film of ink is transferred to the paper;

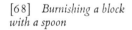
[68] *Burnishing a block with a spoon*

other parts may be burnished heavily to produce a dense black. Textures may be obtained by deliberately uneven burnishing of certain areas. An area may be lightly rubbed all over and then the burnisher may be rubbed heavily in distinct lines to produce dark lines on grey in the resulting print.

If a press is available, it is often a good thing to pass the block through the press and then, before removing the print from the block, burnish selected areas to give greater sharpness or intensity to those parts. Burnishing can only be done effectively with thin papers. Though a thin card is usually placed between burnisher and paper, if care is taken it may be dispensed with and the paper burnished direct. Care must be taken to prevent the burnisher puncturing the paper in the white areas. It is best to press lightly with the hand until the main shapes of the design are visible (as they soon will be with the thin papers used) and then heavier burnishing can be done without fear of piercing the paper in an invisible hollow.

THE BURNISHER   This may be purchased in the form shown in Fig. 69. It is a smooth, rounded, stainless steel tool, set in a wooden handle. But any

[69]   *Burnisher*

hard, smooth, rounded instrument will do, so long as it will slide to and fro under pressure without tearing the paper. For example, a spoon, a book-binder's bone folder, a closed penknife, a toothbrush handle, an illumina-tor's or gilder's agate burnisher.

[70]   *Diagram showing thin card between print and spoon when burnishing*

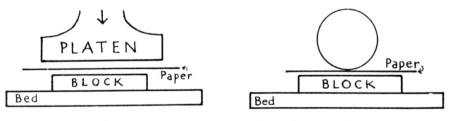

PRESSES   These may be of two main kinds: (1) Platen presses where the pressure is applied by means of a flat slab of metal which may be operated by hand or machine. (2) Cylinder presses where the pressure is applied by a cylinder which also may be power or hand operated.

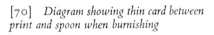

[71]   *Principle of the platen press*   [72]   *Principle of the cylinder press*

PLATEN PRESSES   Perhaps the most familiar of the hand-operated platen presses, suitable for artists to have in home or studio, are the Albion and the Columbian. The latter is delightfully depicted in the engraving by Derrick Harris on page 102. The mechanical principle of the Albion type of press is made clear by the simplified diagram Fig. 74. The block rests on the bed, which is made to run on rails until it is under the platen. This is made to descend by pulling a lever which moves a toggle forcing a wedge into an upright position. The wedge acts on the platen, compelling it to descend with great force. In an Albion press a strong spring lifts the platen again. In the Columbian press a system of levers provides the force to lower the platen, which is lifted again by a lever and counter-weight in the form of an eagle.

The tympan, which is shown on the diagram in dotted lines, is of vellum stretched like a drum, tightly on a metal frame which is hinged to the bed

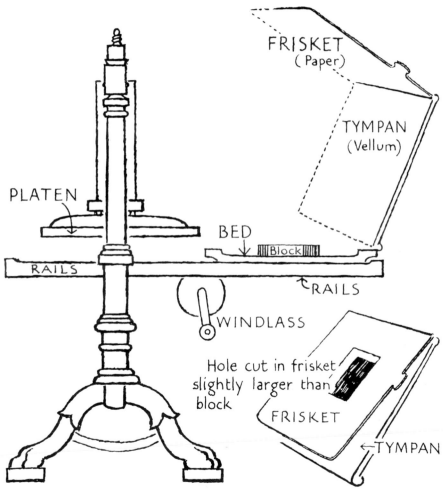

[73]   *Diagram of Albion press giving names of the main parts*

of the press. Hinged to the tympan frame is the frisket, which is a metal frame covered with paper. The tympan and frisket are used when accurate 'register' is required in colour printing or when a series of prints are required with the block printing in exactly the same relative position on each sheet of paper.

Gauge pins or guides made of strips of wood or cardboard are stuck on the tympan so that each sheet of paper can be placed against these guides. To prevent the paper falling off as the typman is turned down onto the block, the frisket is used. A print from the block is made on the frisket and a hole cut the same shape as the print, but very slightly larger. This leaves the paper for the print exposed to the block, while the frisket protects the margins from being soiled, as well as preventing the paper from falling off as the tympan is lowered on to the block.

The windlass turns a drum to which straps are attached that are fixed to each end of the bed. As the drum is revolved by means of the handle, the bed is propelled along the rails under the platen and back again.

The serious engraver would be well advised to invest in an Albion press. It is doubtful if any Albion presses are being made today but they are still obtainable secondhand, direct from printers who may be re-equipping, through Printers Supplies Merchants, or from other craftsmen. Presses for sale are advertised in the printing trade journals and 'Sales & Wants Weekly'. A press a century old may still be in perfect working order.

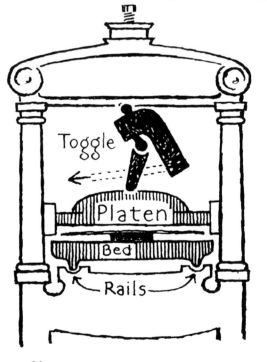

[74] *Mechanical principle of the application of pressure in an Albion press*

Albion presses weigh from ½ cwt. upwards according to size, but they
are not too heavy or too bulky to go in most artists' homes or studios. A
press with a platen 11″ by 16″ requires floor space about two feet by four feet
and weighs about 4 cwt.

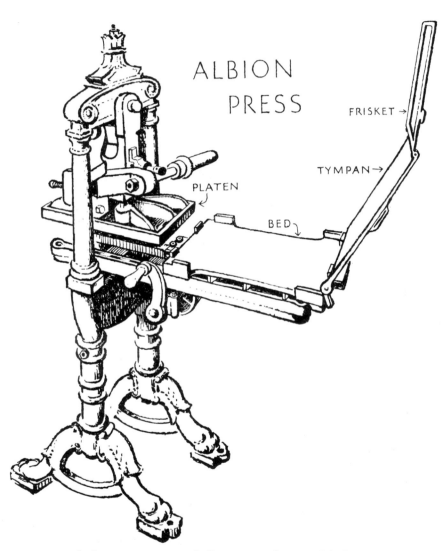

ALBION
PRESS

FRISKET →

TYMPAN →

PLATEN

BED

[75]   *Perspective view of Albion press with names of chief parts*

67

CYLINDER PRESSES These presses have certain mechanical advantages over platens. With platen presses the pressure is applied all over the printing area at the same time. With a cylinder press the pressure is applied in a narrow zone where the cylinder comes into contact with the horizontal paper and block. This narrow zone of pressure moves across the block as the cylinder revolves. A much greater pressure can be maintained over this comparatively small area than is practicable over the whole of the area of a platen. Cylinder presses are therefore much better for printing large blocks. But the cylinder presses which printers use are usually too complex and heavy and too expensive for artist-craftsmen. The type of press which some artists favour for printing large lino-cuts is an etching press.

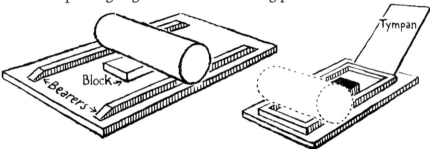

[76] *Bearers and tympan fitted to bed of etching press to make such a press suitable for printing wood blocks*

The mechanical principle is shown in Fig. 72. A steel bed runs under a heavy steel roller whose pressure can be increased by means of a screw, rather like a mangle. As an etching press is designed to print copper plates which, together with the thickness of the blankets, are not usually much more than a quarter of an inch thick, the roller must be lifted to accommodate type-high blocks. This may be done by fixing type-high steel bearers along the sides of bed to support each end of the roller. If desired, a tympan could be constructed and hinged to the bearers as in Fig. 76.

[77] *Placing of strips of lino as bearers when printing a linocut on an etching press. It is often advisable to have bearers when printing on an Albion or on a screw press, too*

When printing linocuts on an etching press, place strips of plain (not inked) linoleum to act as bearers all round the block to be printed. Strips about an inch wide are sufficient on either side but it is wiser to have pieces about three inches wide at the ends which take the first impact of the roller (Fig. 77).

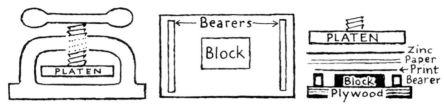

[78]   *Screw press showing section; plan of bed; and section of bed, block, print, etc.*

THE SCREW PRESS   This is not so good as an Albion or a cylinder press, but it is better than none at all. The press consists of a metal bed, above which a thick metal plate (platen) is made to rise and fall by means of a screw. Such a press can often be bought quite cheaply from secondhand shops, particularly those which deal in office equipment.

With this kind of press it is difficult to control the pressure. Bearers used should be of the same height as the block being printed, otherwise it is liable to be damaged. For example, if type-high woodengravings are being printed a strip of type-high metal should be placed at each end of the platen. The block to be printed should be placed centrally under the platen. This is made easier (which also facilitates putting the inked block and paper into the press and taking them out again) by having a piece of plywood (say $\frac{5}{8}''$) the same size as the platen. On this board the block can be placed after inking, together with bearers and a sheet of paper. On top of that it is advisable to place a few more sheets of paper and a sheet of zinc about $\frac{1}{16}''$ thick. The whole can then be placed centrally in the press.

The production of a good print depends on a number of things, the chief of which are (1) the right paper, (2) the right ink, adequately rolled on the slab, and a film of the right thickness transferred to the block, (3) the right amount of pressure in the right places. Paper and ink are dealt with more fully elsewhere; here we will discuss some of the means of controlling pressure. This is called 'make-ready' and is generally of two kinds, underlay and overlay. A third, 'interlay', is possible for linocuts, where paper may be inserted between the lino and the mount.

UNDERLAY in which sheets of paper are stuck *under* the block to make it uniform in height. This is tested by means of a type-high gauge, which is a piece of wood with a slot cut in it exactly the height of type. When this is slipped over the edge of the block it should just go on without too much friction. If it is loose, it is a sign the block is under height at that point and one or more pieces of paper should be stuck on until the gauge feels the same degree of tightness all round the block. The block can then be assumed to be level.

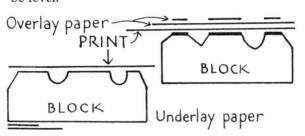

[79] *Section showing placing of paper in underlay and overlay*

OVERLAY   This is the process of varying the amount of pressure by means of different thicknesses of paper at the back of the print. Solids require a greater thickness of paper (which gives more pressure) than do light areas. A more thorough way of doing this is to take three prints and to cut out the solid blacks from one print and to stick them in the corresponding place on another print. From the third print cut out the light areas and stick it precisely on top of the other. The result is a three-ply overlay in which the light areas will get the pressure of one thickness of paper, the middle tones that of two thicknesses, and the solids will receive the pressure of three thicknesses of paper. The paper used for the overlays should generally be fairly thin and soft. Careful tearing of the shapes is better than cutting, which is liable to print as an abrupt change of tone. If the shapes are cut, the edges can be softened by paring with a knife or razor blade or by rubbing with glass-paper. The very darkest areas may require more than two extra thicknesses of paper—the number of sheets required can only be judged by trial and error. More layers of thin paper are better than fewer layers of thick paper. The transition from many layers to the few layers should be gradual. If a series of uniform prints is being made, this overlay is pasted on the tympan, platen or cylinder (according to the kind of press being used) so that it coincides with the block when an impression is being made. In practice it is better if the overlay is not immediately behind the printing paper as the shapes of the different layers of the overlay are liable to show in the print. It is better to bury the overlay under two or three sheets of paper known as packing. It must be understood that the block must be 'locked up' or wedged in the bed of the press so that it cannot move during printing, otherwise the overlay would be useless.

When only a few prints are required, or the press is without tympan or other means of fixing an overlay, prints can be improved by tearing (not cutting) a piece of paper to approximately the shape and size of the area requiring extra pressure and laying it on the back of the print before passing it through the press. If it is difficult to judge the position of the solids from the back, pass the print through the press and the main shapes of the design will usually be visible from the back. Then place the overlay in position and pass through the press again.

The varying tones possible by means of overlays can be exploited as they were in the famous edition of 'Hamlet' from woodcuts by Gordon Craig, printed at Count Kessler's Cranach Press in Weimar (1930). Craig was in daily consultation at the Cranach Press to ensure perfection. A solid uncut block can be made to yield mysterious tones by means of overlays as demonstrated in Fig. 18.

A very good printer once said, 'You print with pressure—not with ink'. An obvious overstatement which nevertheless embodies a sound idea to have in mind. As a matter of routine, always make sure that pressure is correct before worrying about the inking. Test this in the first few prints (or

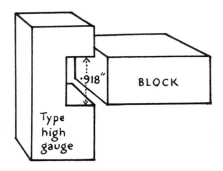

[80]   *An easily made type-high gauge with which to check the thickness of blocks. Blocks should be the same thickness all over. Hard wood should be used for the type-high gauge. The wood 'furniture' that printers use is excellent for this purpose*

pulls as proofs are often called) by examining the back to make sure that the slight embossing is even all over. Once the pressure is made uniformly even, any irregularity in the print must be due to irregularity in the inking.

Whether an accurately cut overlay is used or not, a few sheets of paper, referred to as packing, should always be placed at the back of the print when printing in a press. The number of sheets of packing, which may be hard or soft, will depend on (1) the size of the block, (2) whether the engraving is largely composed of open lines or close fine hatching, (3) the thickness and nature of the paper being printed on. A few experimental prints will show whether a number of sheets of soft pulpy packing such as blotting paper or newsprint yields a better print than a hard packing of manilla or hard-sized cartridge paper. Other things being equal, a hard packing is better when there are a lot of fine white lines. A soft packing has the advantage of adjusting itself to any slight unevenness in the block or in the paper but tends to force the printing paper into the lines and hollows of the block. This makes black lines print more heavily and fine white lines tend to become choked. The resulting increase in tone can sometimes be very considerable and can ruin a design. A good print needs not only a good engraver but a good printer.

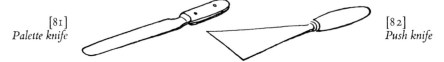

[81]
Palette knife

[82]
Push knife

PALETTE KNIVES If ink is kept in a tin, a palette knife is necessary to remove it when required. But even if the ink is kept in a tube and can therefore be squeezed direct onto the slab, it is best to 'knead' or 'work' the ink with a palette knife before rolling. It is at this stage that varnish, tinting medium, etc., may be added and mixed thoroughly with the palette knife. Two kinds of knife are recommended: one with a flexible blade about six inches long (Fig. 81) which is convenient for removing ink from the tin and for mixing small quantities of ink. Large quantities of ink can be mixed better with a push-knife which has a stiffer blade (Fig. 82). A useful size has a blade about 3″ across. A push-knife saves a lot of time in cleaning up the slab as it will scrape a zone three inches wide at one stroke. A few strokes will scrape most of the thick ink into a heap which can then be picked up and put on to scrap paper and thrown in the waste bin. A large waste bin is most desirable, particularly one with a wide opening.

72

INKING THE BLOCK   After the ink has been thoroughly rolled on the slab it should immediately be rolled on the block. Remember that as soon as rolling stops the ink tends to loose some of its fluidity, tends to oxidize, tends to get tacky. The rolling of the block should be systematic—not haphazard, and should be conditioned by the size of the block and the nature of the engraving. A satisfactory system with a large block is to start in the middle and roll diagonally outwards across each corner in turn. Then roll up and down the length of the block. If the roller projects over the edges of the block, once or twice up and down might be enough; but if the block is wider than the roller, the rolling must be repeated to cover the whole area. With a large block it may be necessary to pick up more ink from the slab; if so, roll lightly many times on the block to make sure the ink is evenly distributed. The amount of rolling and the quantity of ink required on the roller will vary with the block and the absorbency of the paper, and these may be judged by experience.

When rolling on the slab no harm is done by exerting a certain amount of pressure, but on the block the weight of the roller alone is sufficient to transfer the ink and a little too much pressure will force the ink into the fine white lines and choke them. Small blocks, say 1″ square, may be held in the hand and rolled with the other. Some people find it easier to avoid too much pressure in this way. Large blocks must, of course, be inked while resting on the bed of the press or other flat surface.

ROLLERS   These are best if made of the composition usually used for rollers on printing machines but plastic rollers are now available which have most of the advantages and few of the drawbacks of the traditional 'composition'.

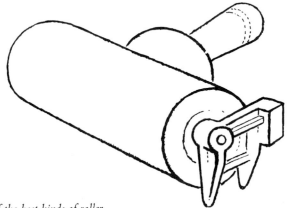

[83]   *One of the best kinds of roller*

Composition rollers must not be allowed to get hot otherwise they will melt; nor must they ever be left resting on the ink slab because this will flatten the part of the roller left in contact with the slab. The best kind of roller frame, therefore, is the kind illustrated on page 73, which has four little legs which keep the composition part of the roller just clear of the slab. Those frames without the legs necessitate being placed on their backs to prevent the roller resting on the slab when not in use, and therefore need extra bench space alongside the ink slab. For general purposes a roller six inches wide and about three inches in diameter is most serviceable. Rollers with a smaller diameter have the disadvantage of carrying less ink. When inking a large block, it follows that after the roller has made one complete revolution it will deposit considerably less ink than during its first revolution. Unless the roller is passed to and fro many times in different directions the area beyond the first revolution of the roller will show as a lighter tone owing to the thinner deposit of ink.

Nowhere near as good, but considerably cheaper, are 'squeegee' rollers which have a wooden core on which is a smooth rubber 'tyre'. These are usually of small diameter and are not resilient like the plastic and composition rollers.

Rollers should always be cleaned immediately after use. Ink should never be allowed to dry on them. The most serviceable solvent is ordinary paraffin which is cheap, and safe to store. Petrol is, of course, an efficient solvent for normal oil printing inks but has the disadvantage of being dangerously inflammable and rapidly evaporates, leaving a hard deposit if, by chance, cleaning operations are interrupted. Turps substitute (white spirit) is also an effectual cleaning fluid.

Good craftsmen are usually neat and tidy in all stages of work, even in cleaning up. Method saves time and mess. A good method of cleaning ink slab and roller(s) is as follows. An old telephone directory provides a conveniently sized stock of sheets of absorbent waste paper (but newspapers would do). First sprinkle the ink slab with paraffin. (A special sprinkler can

[84] *Paraffin sprinkler*

[85] *Ink dabber*

74

is sold for this purpose but an old oilcan is quite efficient.) Then roll the paraffin all over the slab until the ink on both slab and roller is very runny. Place two or three sheets of paper on the slab and run the roller to and fro over them. The paper will absorb the diluted ink from roller and slab. Lift

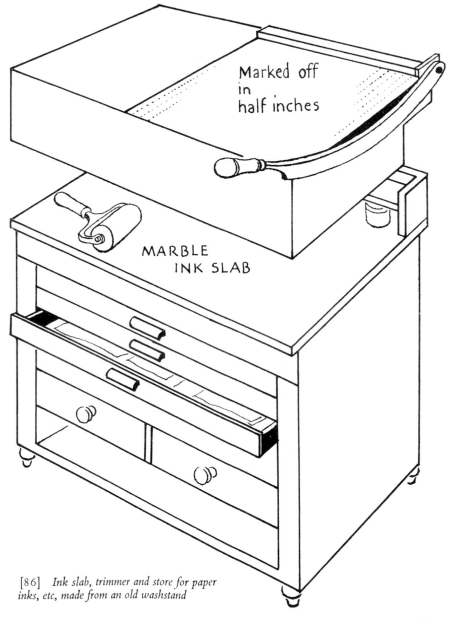

Marked off
in
half inches

MARBLE
INK SLAB

[86]   *Ink slab, trimmer and store for paper inks, etc, made from an old washstand*

up the top sheet and turn it, dirty side down, on to the sheet underneath, leaving the clean side to grasp in the hand. Screwing up the paper slightly, it can then be used to wipe the slab without dirtying the hands. A good crafts-man is not afraid of dirtying his hands, but he does not make them messy unnecessarily. Repeat the operation once more with paper (that is if there is much ink still left) and finish off with rag.

Composition rollers respond to the humidity of the air by swelling in damp air and shrinking in dry air. If the air is very dry and the rollers are hard, a quick wipe with a damp but not wet rag will resuscitate them. Never leave them in a damp place. It is best to keep them under cover.

An alternative to a roller, though by no means as easy to handle, is a dab-ber such as the early printers used. This is mushroom shaped and is made of fairly thin flexible leather stuffed with rags or cotton wool (Fig. 85).

INK SLAB Special inking tables are used in the printing trade, but the artist-printer can rarely afford such luxuries. But quite as good, if not better, is a marble slab. An old washstand with a marble top makes an almost ideal ink slab. The author has fitted up an old washstand with drawers to store blocks, paper, etc., as shown in Fig. 86. The cover is made of $\frac{5}{8}''$ by $8''$ deal for the sides and plywood for the top. A guillotine is fixed to the top which is ruled with lines half an inch apart to make the trimming of paper quicker and more accurate.

While ink is on the slab it is best to replace the cover, even during a lunch break, to prevent dust settling and fouling the ink.

Old litho-stones also make good ink slabs, as do thick sheets of glass. White paper under the glass makes it easier to judge the hue and tone when mixing colours. Sheet zinc or aluminium is quite satisfactory and can be used to cover the top of an old washstand, table or cupboard of the right height. This may be stuck on with one of the 'Bostik' or other synthetic adhesives; or, alternatively, bent over at the edges and fixed with screws at the sides—not on the top.

[87] EARLY
NINETEENTH-CENTURY
TRADE ENGRAVING
Printed from the wood

Whatever the slab is made of it should be smooth, non-absorbent, and on a rigid base.

OIL INKS   The inks used for printing woodengravings are fundamentally the same as those used by trade printers, that is, they are mainly composed of a pigment or colouring matter mixed with boiled linseed oil. They are sold in tins or tubes. Tubes are a little more expensive, but, being more airtight than tins, the ink in them can be kept for years without a thick, wasteful skin forming. Screw caps should always be replaced immediately after use otherwise the ink will go hard in the neck of the tube. The thickest inks are best kept in tins. The surface of the ink should be kept covered with grease-proof or oiled paper. When removing ink, the paper should be lifted and ink taken from the top, keeping the surface as level as possible. Do not dig a hole in the ink as this exposes a large area to the air, forming a skin. If the ink has previously been dug out carelessly it becomes very difficult to remove ink without including offensive crumbs of hard skin.

It is advisable to have more than one kind of black ink. A good 'halftone black' is excellent for finely engraved work. This is the ink printers use to print 'half-tone' blocks. A wide variety of colours is available; the yellows are opaque; the reds and blues are more transparent. White is usually very opaque, but a more or less transparent white is now sold. Tinting medium or 'Tinteen' added to a colour produces a paler tint. Driers can be mixed with the ink to hasten drying, but they are liable to spoil the quality of the ink. Nowadays the manufacture of inks is a highly specialized business, requiring a considerable knowledge of chemistry, but the artist can trust a reputable ink-maker to provide him with good durable inks so long as he pays a good price. Cheap inks are an abomination. Inks vary considerably in density or covering power. Black inks vary greatly in 'colour': some have a warm, brownish tinge, some are cool and bluish, others are greenish. The shade of ink should be chosen to suit the nature of the picture or design.

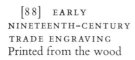

[88] EARLY NINETEENTH-CENTURY TRADE ENGRAVING Printed from the wood

[89] NINETEENTH-CENTURY TRADE ENGRAVING Printed from the wood

Generally speaking, the stiffer the ink the better. But inks must suit the paper to be printed on, and sometimes this means thinning or softening the ink. If the ink is too stiff and sticky and the paper has a loose surface, when the print is lifted from the block some of the surface of the paper will be found sticking to the block instead of the ink being transferred to the print. This 'picking' of the paper surface can be prevented by 'reducing' the ink with a few spots of paraffin, a little varnish (as supplied by ink manufacturers—not house painters' varnish), a little vaseline, or a little reducing medium—which is supplied by the ink manufacturers. Only by experience can one learn to judge when an ink needs reducing and how much is required. If in doubt, the safest rule is not to adulterate in any way the ink as supplied by the maker.

The following manufacturers can be relied upon for a good ink: Winston's, Lorilleux & Bolton, Mander Bros., Shackell Edwards & Co. Most makers have an ink known as 'Handpress Black' or by some similar name. This is stiff, very black, does not dry quickly on the slab but will dry reasonably quickly on the paper. For very little extra charge ink makers will mix a special ink to the requirements of a customer. If a special ink is required it is best to send the manufacturer a specimen of the paper or papers it is proposed to print on and tell him, if possible, the working conditions and the properties it is desirable the ink should have. But no one ink is ideal for all papers and in all conditions.

Inks dry in three ways: (1) by absorption into the paper; (2) by evaporation whereby the 'vehicle' in the ink evaporates, leaving the pigment behind on the paper; (3) by oxidation or other chemical change that occurs when a thin

78

[90] NINETEENTH-CENTURY TRADE ENGRAVING Printed from the wood

film of ink is exposed to the air. If the paper is hard-sized and therefore not readily absorbent, the ink will not dry unless its chemical composition lends itself to oxidation and evaporation.

The quantity of ink required to print efficiently varies with the absorbency of the paper. Soft sized or waterleaf (unsized) papers require considerably more ink on the block than is necessary for hard papers. Again, only by experience or trial and error can the correct amount of ink be judged. Do not over-ink. It is better to have only a moderate amount of ink spread out on the slab and to roll on the slab and then over the block twice, rather than to have a larger amount of ink on the slab and roll the block once over. This might produce over-inking. Too much ink on the roller at one time is liable to choke the fine white lines with the first roll, even though the blacks may be solid.

Inks have the physical property of behaving like solids when stationary, as in the tin; but behaving like fluids when agitated, as when stirred or rolled to and fro. The more the ink is rolled to and fro on the slab the more fluid the ink will tend to be (within limits) and in consequence it will spread more easily and evenly on the block. It is always worth while rolling out the ink very thoroughly before attempting to transfer any of the ink to the block. It is best to spread a supply of ink in a sort of long low mound across the slab slightly longer than the width of the roller. This is better than one heap which transfers a blob of ink to the roller which must be rolled many times before the ink is evenly distributed. The long low mound enables the roller

79

to pick up a fresh supply of ink along the whole of its length. Roll in many directions. Lift the roller and allow it to spin now and then. When the ink is in the right condition for printing, the surface of the ink will glisten like smooth satin and be completely free from dust and specks of dirt or dried ink. The sound the roller makes is also a guide. It should hiss pleasantly, not sloppily or stickily, but musically like the suck of the sea on sand.

WATER INKS The oil inks described for use with woodengravings can be used for woodcuts and all the hints given on the foregoing pages apply to woodcuts just as to woodengraving. But water inks are often used for woodcuts whether in the traditional Japanese manner or in the contemporary idiom. These may be bought ready mixed in tins or tubes. Water inks may be diluted with water to a very pale tint or left at full strength. A tinting medium can be used which also reduces the strength of the hue but gives more body to the ink than when reduced with water only. White added to a colour makes a lighter tone but also alters the hue to some extent. It is also opaque, which gives a different quality to the print. The makers claim that all colours mix safely with one another. A little glycerine helps to keep water ink soft and moist. Some colours are more intense and have more covering power than others. Some colours print smoothly and easily while others are more gritty or tend to print with a mottled effect. This mottled effect may be a drawback or it may be exploited and made an integral part of the design. Yellows are usually opaque and will tend to obliterate any colour it prints upon; most blues and reds are transparent and will therefore allow any underprinting to show through to a certain extent.

The Japanese inks are composed of powder colour mixed with rice-paste. The most finely ground powders are best, and can be obtained from an artists' colour-man. The rice paste is made from rice flour and is best made fresh every day. It is made by soaking rice flour in water overnight, making sure water is stirred in well to form a smooth, lump-free paste. More water is added to it in a saucepan and brought slowly to the boil, stirring con-

[91] VAN GELDER *Decoration* Engraving, actual size (Dutch)

stantly. Just before the whole of the mixture turns translucent it should be poured off into another vessel ready for use. Saucers, plates or small cake tins will serve for mixing a little of the paste with the powder colour and as much water as is required for the desired tone. The rice (starch) paste gives body

[92]   MORGENS ZIELER   *Highland Cattle*   Linocut, 20½ by 8⅝ inches (Danish)

to the pigment and, being slightly adhesive, the paper will stick to the block sufficiently to avoid slipping while being burnished on the back of the print. REGISTER   When all the blocks from which a colour print is made are printed in correct relation to one another, they are said to be 'in register'. The marks or guides on the blocks to make precise register possible are known as register marks. Whether or not the colours in the final print register correctly depends first on the accuracy with which the blocks are cut. Not only must the parts of the design to be printed in different colours be cut in accurate relationship to one another, but the register marks on each block must be in the same relationship to the design.

There are many methods of obtaining register. The chief and most reliable methods will be described, but the enterprising engraver may well devise other methods to suit his own temperament, conditions and equipment.

The method employed will depend largely on the nature of the design. If the design demands precise 'pin point' register, then a precise method must be used; but if the design is such that it will not be harmed if certain colours are a little out of register, easier, if less accurate, methods of register can be used. Some people regard the slight inaccuracies of register, so often encountered in hand-made prints, as part of the character and beauty of colour prints. Sometimes this is true, but the 'inaccuracies' of register should be conscious and contrived, not accidental as the result of inability to make blocks register with one another. Nevertheless, freedom, looseness even, is preferable to a soulless mechanical accuracy.

Perhaps the simplest method is that in which the design is so arranged that one of the colours forms a skeleton of the whole design. This skeleton or 'key' block as it is called, is cut first, the drawing being transferred to the block by one of the methods described on page 59. If prints are ultimately to be made on a press with which register can be obtained on the tympan or cylinder, no register marks will be necessary on the block, but they are essential if the prints are to be taken by hand. Register marks are notches cut

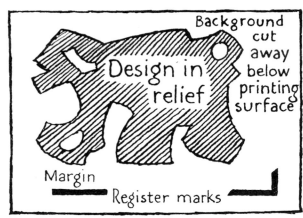

[93] *Plan of block showing placing of register marks*

in the block at a sufficient distance from the edge of the design to allow for adequate margins (Fig. 93). It will be seen that the block is appreciably larger than the design and as this means a large area of 'waste', this method is generally used for wood-cutting and lino-cutting for which the material is cheap compared with the cost of boxwood. Fig. 94 shows that the register mark is a notch which has a vertical side on the register line (or 'lay-edge', which is the correct technical term) and slopes up into the marginal space. Register marks should always be cut on the longest side of the block. The position corresponds to the position of the thumbs when laying the paper on the block as shown in the diagram on page 83. The paper, of course, should fit snugly against the register mark, with no 'play' at all, at every impression.

When the design and register marks are cut and sufficient of the background removed, a proof should be taken. The amount of background taken away depends on the method of printing and inking. If inking is being done with a brush in the Japanese manner, just sufficient background can be cut away to avoid any unwanted surface being inked. The un-inked but still raised parts will help to support the paper, which will almost certainly be damp and rather fragile. If the block is being inked by rollers it is obvious that all parts not required to print must be cut away well below the printing surface.

PAPER

REGISTER MARK

Inked printing surface

[94] *Section of register mark*

Assuming the proof of the key block is correct, including the placing and proofing of the register marks, the proof, while still wet, should be placed, inked side down, onto the block prepared for the second colour and passed through a press (or burnished as the case may be) so that a set-off of the print

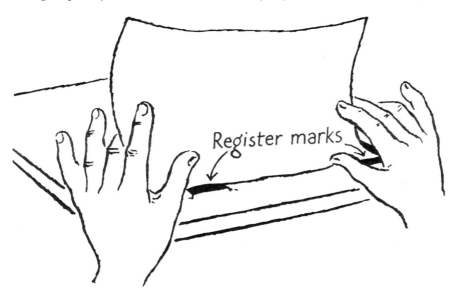

Register marks

[95] *Method of holding paper when placing against register marks*

is made upon the second block. A further proof and a further set-off must be made for every other colour block required. On each of these blocks the background must be cut away, leaving only the register marks and those parts required to print in the colour for which the block is intended. Make sure the register marks are accurately cut. It is wise to cut them first lest they be cut away by mistake in clearing the background.

It is not always necessary to cut a whole block for every colour. Areas of different colour that are far enough apart to be inked without brushing or rolling one colour into the other may be cut on one block.

The register marks are, indeed, only for making the set-offs from the key block; after that, the design only is inked, leaving the register marks clean.

In the method we have described it has been assumed that the 'key' block is reasonably complete in itself, like a skeleton requiring only to be clothed with the flesh of colour to give it 'body'. To change the simile, the 'key' is like a map, within the contours of which the colours may be placed, though some areas of colour may overlap, giving additional colours. This is simple to do and for many beginners it is the best way of branching out from black and white into colour prints. But many artists do not think of their pictures in this way. They think of masses of colour juxtaposed and overlapping without the support of a skeleton 'key'. Indeed such a way of looking at things is possibly more in keeping with the spirit of art at the present time. Nevertheless a key drawing will be needed in order to make sure that the shapes cut on different blocks will finally print in true relation to one another.

A tracing of all the main lines of the design must be made and register marks indicated. The register marks must be traced onto every block. Then each block must have traced upon it only those shapes required to be in the colour for which the individual block is intended, e.g. red shapes on one block, yellow shapes on another block, and so on. If precise register is required very great care must be taken to trace extremely accurately and to guard against the stretching of the paper. If there is a danger of some of the parts of the design not fitting exactly it is best during the cutting to leave those parts slightly large until a proof has been taken. Then such refinements as are considered necessary can be made, bearing in mind that a shape may be reduced in size by cutting away wood, but nothing can be added. Register marks must, of course, be cut *very* accurately.

A method of registering woodengravings is to glue, base uppermost on a board, two old engravings so that they lie at right angles to one another. We shall call them 'lay' blocks. It is best if one of these blocks is just the width of the proposed margins—if not, a line can be drawn on the block where the edge of the paper should come. The paper is hinged by means of adhesive tape to the edge of one of the blocks (or to the drawn line). The block is inked

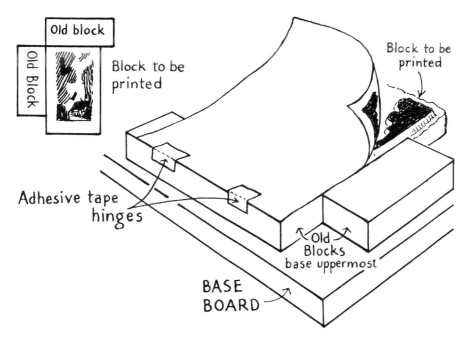

[96] *Method of registering woodengraving by hinging print to old block*

and placed against the two fixed blocks (Fig. 96) and the paper lowered on to it. The print may then be burnished or passed through a press. The paper is lifted (but not removed from its hinges) while the engraved block is removed and a new one put in its place. The print is lowered onto the new block and passed through the press to obtain a 'set-off'. The block is then ready to be engraved for the second colour. Additional set-offs will be required for additional colours. When the desired number of blocks is engraved, multi-colour prints are obtained by going through a similar procedure. Namely, the paper is hinged to one of the lay blocks. The block to be printed is inked, placed against the lay blocks, the paper is lowered and printed. The paper is lifted; the block is removed and another, inked with the second colour, takes its place. The paper is lowered and again printed. This procedure is repeated for as many times as there are blocks to be printed.

The method is reasonably accurate, because once carefully hinged there should not be any longtitudinal or lateral movement of the paper. The drawback is that all the colours on one print must be printed in succession owing to the fact that the paper must remain on its hinges until the print is complete. It means, of course, that there must be as many ink slabs in use at one time as there are colours to be printed. It is a convenient method for proofing designs in two or three colours that are ultimately to be printed on a press.

If the design is squared up, that is, if it occupies an exact rectangle with a line forming the boundary of the rectangle, a very simple method of register is possible. After the first 'key' block is cut a proof is trimmed to the very edge of the print. This is laid, ink side down, on a new block (which should, of course, be the exact size of the print) and passed through the press to obtain a set-off. When all blocks have been engraved or cut, an edition of prints can be taken in the following way.

The placing on the paper of the first block can be 'by eye', that is to say the paper may be laid on the inked block by hand without any mechanical aids to placing, because in this method of register uniform margins are not essential. When the edition in one colour has been printed, the next block is inked. This time, instead of laying the paper on the block, the block is laid on the paper. The proceedure is as follows. The print is laid on a few sheets of packing on the bed of the press. The block should be inked and picked up carefully. With the inked surface underneath, gently lower the block until a corner is in contact with a corner of the print. Then lower the whole of the longest side, being careful to see that the edge of the block coincides exactly with the edge of the first print. As soon as the whole of the edge of the block is in contact with the edge of the print, drop the rest of the block, but do not allow it to slip out of alignment with the print. It is then passed through the press and if the block has been laid without mishap, the two colours should be in register. The same process is repeated for each succeeding colour.

It is evident that some manual dexterity is required to lay the block into position without slurring, and it is advisable to practise the movements with an uninked block, placing it on scrap paper until sufficient skill and confidence is obtained. This should not take long—at least with small blocks. Large blocks are more difficult to lay accurately.

This method, though easy with a squared-up block, is not possible with an irregular design, nor is it accurate enough for very precise register.

Unmounted linocuts may be registered in the following way. Cut two strips of cardboard, slightly thinner than the lino, and stick at right angles onto a board (Fig. 97). Rubber solution is one of the best adhesives as it allows of some manipulation and movement before final sticking. But a clean and convenient method of sticking the strip of cardboard to the mount is by adhesive tape, preferably of the 'Sellotape' variety. Be careful to see that the tape is tucked well into the angle between the base and the cardboard to

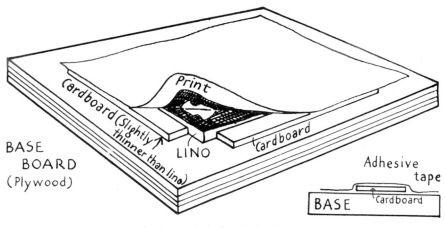

[97] *Method of registering linocuts*

form a right angle. The strips of cardboard should be as wide as the margins of the print are intended to be because the edges of the paper will be laid to coincide with the edges of the cardboard.

The lino to be printed is inked and placed against these two strips of cardboard. The paper is laid so that two edges coincide with the outer edges of the strips of cardboard and then gently lowered onto the linoleum. A print is then taken either by burnishing or in a press.

The number of prints that may be taken from one block will vary according to the nature of the design, but as many as 750,000 satisfactory prints have been taken from one engraving.

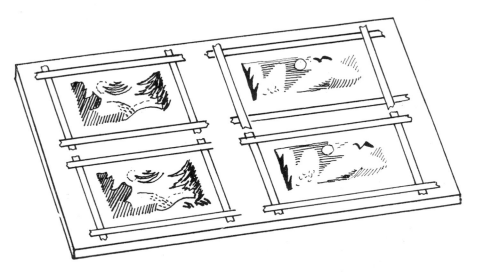

[98] *Damp prints laid out and stuck with adhesive tape while drying*

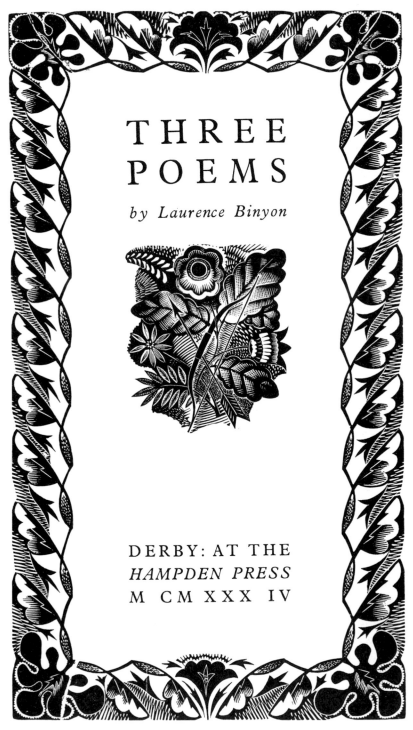

THREE
POEMS

by Laurence Binyon

DERBY: AT THE
HAMPDEN PRESS
M CM XXX IV

[99]   JOHN R. BIGGS   *Border and ornament for title page*   Engraving, from the wood

PAPER

IT IS IMPORTANT to remember that paper is part of the picture—sometimes a very considerable part—and the quality of a print depends to a certain extent on the character of the paper. Except for rough proofs, only papers having the purest ingredients should be used. These will endure.

The word paper is derived from papyrus, a kind of sedge which grew abundantly by the Nile. It was made into sheets for writing on by cutting the stems lengthwise into strips which were laid side by side and supported by another similar layer of strips laid at right angles to the first layer. It was used by the early Egyptians and Greeks, who make the papyrus in long bands which were rolled on sticks to form 'books'. Modern paper is made of cellulose derived from various plants by tearing the fibres apart and then adding sufficient water to make the 'stuff'* flow easily over a wire mould to form a continuous sheet or web of paper of uniform thickness. Most, but by no means all, of the best papers for printing woodcuts, woodengravings and lino-cuts are handmade.

Paper merchants refer to the thickness of paper in terms of weight per ream of a given size. Thus a paper may be referred to as crown 40 lbs. or crown 60 lbs., which means that a ream (480 or 500 sheets) of the first paper weighs 40 lbs., a ream of the second weights 60 lbs. and therefore must be thicker than the first. That is, if it is the same kind of paper. It is obvious that art-paper (which is coated with china clay) will be heavier than a similar bulk of blotting paper.

Smooth, fairly soft papers are best for printing engravings composed of very fine white lines. Hard, rough papers are very difficult to print on because without great pressure the ink will not reach the bottom of the minute hollows with which the surface of such papers abounds. Damping the paper softens the surface and allows areas of 'solid' ink to be printed, but there is a tendency for fine white lines to fill in and the print as a whole will appear

---

*Stuff is the correct technical term.

heavier than when printed on a smoother dry paper. A press is required for printing on rough, hard papers. Burnishing can only be done effectively on thin, fairly soft papers.

JAPANESE PAPERS These are, perhaps, the best of all for hand-proofs, whether taken by burnishing or on a press. There is a very wide range of Japanese papers. There is white, thin tissue which is transparent and astonishingly strong in spite of its thinness. At the other extreme there is thick, opaque, creamy coloured paper. In between there are many different thicknesses, different shades of cream, white and off-white, different degrees of opacity. Some are smooth and of uniform thickness, some have an irregular crazy network of clumps of fibre that are appreciably thicker than the spaces in between. Some have tiny specks of dark material scattered over the paper, some are practically unblemished. Some have a vellum or parchment-like surface.

The best Japanese papers are made from the fibres of the mulberry tree. Japanese artists have favoured Hōsho, a paper made from the bark of kōzo (paper mulberry). From early times this paper, more than any other, has been used in Japan for making prints. Torinoko is another very good paper. It is made mainly from the bark of gampi (*Wikstraemia*), with the addition of wood pulp or manilla fibre. It is a rich cream in colour, smooth, even and firm and can be obtained in different thicknesses. In England the Japanese names of the papers are rarely used. T. N. Lawrence refers to Japanese papers by number, e.g. No. 15, No. 34. Papers are best chosen by sight and touch —the feel of paper gives a clue to its nature. It is advisable to try a number of different kinds of paper.

INDIA PAPERS These papers are made from the inner fibres of bamboo stems. Some India papers are liable to be blemished by dark spots which, however, may be only on the surface and can be removed with a sharp pointed knife. Other marks go deeper, and cannot be removed. India papers are usually white. Thin 'India' papers are used for printing Bibles and other books where a large number of pages is required in a small bulk. They are suitable for burnished prints.

[100]
This page and opposite: Three decorations by the author

OTHER PAPERS An enterprising artist-craftsman will always be on the lookout for papers of character, or for papers suitable for a particular kind of work and the following are but a few of these.

Basingwerk Parchment, made by Grosvenor Chater, is an excellent smooth silky paper that will print the finest of white lines. It is made in white and cream and other shades and in a variety of thicknesses. *Nippon Vellum* and *Jappon Vellum*, as the name implies, are imitation vellum papers whose smooth, creamy kindly surface is just right for some prints. *Newsprint*, that is, the better qualities of newsprint, are admirable for taking proofs. The surface is smooth and sympathetic and will usually take the finest of lines. Newsprint, being largely composed of wood pulp, deteriorates rapidly by becoming yellow and brittle, particularly if exposed to light, and is therefore not suitable for collector's prints. Another good paper for proofs, but not for collector's or exhibition prints, is *M.F. Printing*. This is smooth, thin and fairly white. Whatever is used for the final prints, a white paper is often advisable for proofs because white tends to show up faults which may then be corrected. Any printer will be able to supply a small quantity of M.F. Printing paper (and a number of other kinds of paper that may be worth trying). *Offset Cartridge*, that is, the paper made for printing offset lithography, has a kindly surface, and a firm feel which is suitable for some subjects. There are many different makes of offset cartridge—and again a printer will probably provide what is wanted. *Cigarette Paper* is a satisfactory though extremely thin white paper, for making prints by burnishing, but care must be taken not to tear the print.

The firms of Whatman, Barcham Green, or Batchelor all supply fine hand-made papers that can be used for prints, and any of the following are equally suitable, e.g. Ingres, Charles I, Michallet, Van Gelder.

Those papers like Ingres and Michallet which are 'laid' (fine parallel lines are visible when held up to the light) are liable to show these lines in the print. Sometimes it is pleasant for large areas of solid ink to be relieved by the texture of the fine lines in the paper, but sometimes this is offensive and may be avoided by using extra pressure in those parts when printing.

[101] WERNER BERG *Owls* cut, 18½ by 9¼ inches (Austrian)

DAMPING We have already said that damping improves the ink-retaining properties of paper. Hard, rough papers are almost impossible to print on satisfactorily unless the paper is damp and some soft papers yield a better print if slightly damp. The paper obviously should not be wet. Old craftsmen said it should be 'dry to the touch but cool to the cheek'.

Damping is best done by carrying out the following procedure. A quantity of blotting paper (or other absorbent paper) is first damped by making a pile of alternate dry and wet sheets. For example, take a piece of zinc or linoleum rather larger than the paper to be damped and on it place two dry sheets of blotting paper. The next sheet of blotting paper is passed through a bowl of water and laid on top of the two dry sheets. Two dry sheets are then laid on top of the wet one, and another sheet is passed through the bowl of water before being added to the pile. This procedure is repeated until the required amount is done. A pile of blotting paper is thus made composed of alternate layers of two dry and one wet sheets. The degree of dampness can be adjusted by having the layers composed of one wet and one dry, or one wet and three dry sheets. Another piece of zinc or linoleum is placed on top of the pile which is kept under pressure until the moisture is evenly distributed through every sheet. Any heavy object on top of the pile will provide the necessary pressure.

The damp sheets of blotting paper and the sheets of dry printing paper are then made into a pile composed of alternate wet and dry sheets, and kept under pressure until the moisture is evenly distributed throughout. This may conveniently be done in the evening and the sheets left under pressure until

[102] JOSEPH CRAWHALL *Illustration* Cut, actual size

the next morning, when they will be ready for printing. If the room is warm, it is advisable to put damp cloth round the edges of the pile, which are otherwise inclined to dry a little. The printing should be carried out immediately and the prints hung up or placed on boards to dry as in diagram 98. Paper left damp in warm rooms is apt to grow moulds rather quickly.

Care must be taken in handling as damp paper is more liable to tear than dry. If colour prints are being made, the paper must be kept damp until the last colour is printed, because paper shrinks as it dries (not always by the same amount in each direction), and if the paper were not kept damp the last colours to be printed would not fit (register) the earlier colours owing to the shrinkage of the paper. It is obviously best to print the colours as quickly as possible one after the other.

As prints dry they sometimes cockle. This can be prevented by laying out each damp print on a board and sticking down the edges. (Fig. 98).

When the print is dry the gummed tape can be lifted from the board and the print trimmed. Prints should never be stored until perfectly dry, otherwise the ink of one print may 'set off' on the back of the print above and the paper may become foxed or grow other moulds that paper is subject to.

Nearly all papers have a 'right' and a 'wrong' side, that is to say one side is usually more smooth than the other. Observe the two sides of the paper carefully and consider which side is likely to print most effectively. The smoothest side is regarded as the 'right' side, but if the other side has a texture which suits the subject to be printed—why not use it?

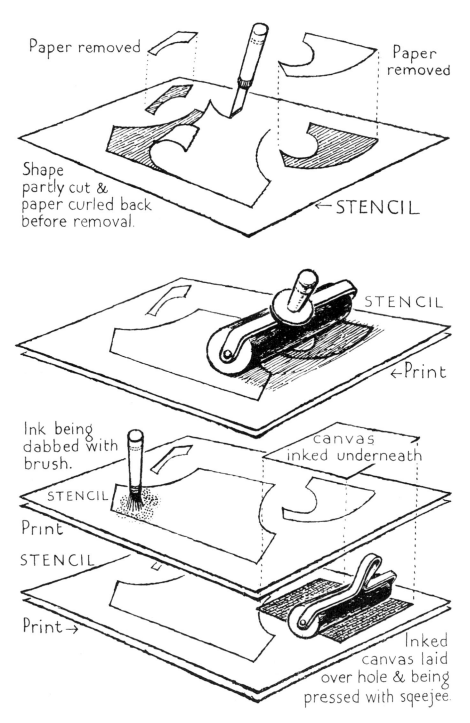

Paper removed

Paper removed

Shape
partly cut &
paper curled back
before removal.

←STENCIL

STENCIL

←Print

Ink being
dabbed with
brush.

STENCIL

canvas
inked underneath

Print

STENCIL

Print→

Inked
canvas laid
over hole & being
pressed with sqeejee.

[103]   *Diagram showing use of stencils*

STENCILLING AND
OTHER METHODS

STENCILLING is here thought of, not as a method on its own of producing images, but as a subsidiary process to add colours to prints that are basically woodcut, linocut or woodengraving.

A stencil is simply a sheet of paper, thin metal or other thin firm material in which holes of the shapes desired may be cut and through which ink may be dabbed or rolled to produce a print.

Stencils are useful where simple, bold shapes are required and for which it might be as extravagant as it would be tedious to cut an additional woodblock. But that is not all: it is possible to obtain effects that could not be obtained in any other way. Remember that a stencil is a mask (of paper or other similar material) that covers the print being made except for those areas that have been cut away revealing the printing paper below. Perhaps the commonest method is to dab ink through the holes with a stiff brush, but it is possible to roll the ink on with the ordinary composition roller.

Instead of dabbing or rolling the ink through the stencil directly onto the print, a variety of effects can be obtained by inking other materials (e.g. Lincrusta Walton, embossed paper, coarse canvas, etc.), laying the inked material over the hole in the stencil and applying pressure by means of a press, by burnishing, or by rolling with a squeejee. An interesting effect may be obtained by screwing up a piece of paper, laying it out flat, rolling ink lightly over it, and then pressing it, ink side down, through the hole in the stencil.

We have said that we are here concerned with stencilling as a means of adding colours to woodcuts or linocuts, and the simplest way of making

[104] ERIC RAVILIOUS *Decoration* Engraving, printed from the wood

95

[105] EDNA WHITE   *The Canterbury Tales*   Cut, actual size

such a stencil is to use a proof of the woodcut. This proof should be on a good strong cartridge paper. The shapes required may be cut in the proof with the woodcutting knife. It is advisable to place a few sheets of newspaper under the proof being cut and to have a sheet of metal or glass under them all while cutting.

Register may be obtained by using the edges of the paper, because, if a print is used to make the stencil, it will therefore have the same margins as the woodcut.

If a large edition is to be printed the paper stencil can be strengthened by varnishing.

We have said that the most satisfactory way of cutting a stencil which is to be used in association with a woodcut or linocut is to use a proof of the woodcut, nevertheless in the final edition of prints the stencil could, if desired, be printed first. Blocks or stencils may be printed in any sequence at the will of the artist. The order of printing can considerably influence the appearance of the finished print.

CUT CARDBOARD   Another way of obtaining relief prints which has been used effectively in America is to cut out in cardboard of convenient thickness —say from one-sixteenth to one-eighth of an inch—the shapes desired and to glue them onto plywood, chip-board or other substance to bring the total thickness to type height. For the cutting, scissors will do where the cardboard is fairly thin and the shapes bold, but a trimming knife or woodcutting knife is better for some shapes.

Only bold shapes are possible in cardboard, but a variety of surface textures is possible. As in other methods of creating printing blocks, a separate block will be required for each colour printed.

It is reasonable to use this method in conjunction with woodcutting, wood-engraving and linocutting when broad, bold shapes are required in a particular colour combined with more detailed work in another colour. It might be expensive and tedious to cut or engrave blocks for shapes that might be

96

equally well cut in cardboard. The diagram (Fig. 106) makes it clear how the cardboard shapes appear when glued to a mount.

MISCELLANEOUS We have described the usual methods of making relief prints but it is possible to obtain prints from any flat surface which will retain ink. It is therefore open to an artist-craftsman to experiment with any material that appeals to him, be it plastic, metal, or wood. Some are capable of being engraved upon, e.g. various plastics and metals, while others can only be cut into simple shapes.

There are effects to be obtained in prints which do not properly come under any of our main headings and are referred to here briefly because they may suggest other ideas to the reader.

An interesting linear effect can be obtained with string in two different ways.

(1) After the block (be it wood or lino) has been inked, the string may be laid in whatever shape the designer wishes on the inked surface, taking care that the string does not wriggle or turn over while laying it in position. The printing paper is then laid on the block and printed in a press in the usual way. The result is a soft-edged white line in the print where the string was.

As the string has to be laid afresh for each print it is evident that two prints could rarely be precisely alike (but perhaps uniformity is not always important) and only small editions would be tolerable.

(2) String may be glued to the overlay (q.v.), in which case the result is a rather darker line with a lighter boundary along the line of the string.

On the same principle, paper-clips, pieces of thin wire, hairs, bristles, etc., may be laid on the block or stuck on the overlay to produce unusual effects.

If the principle of relief printing is fully understood there are surely other ways of producing prints still waiting to be discovered by the questing artist-craftsman.

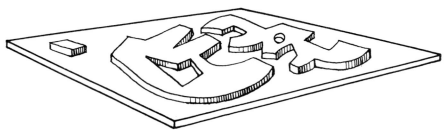

[106] *Printing block made by sticking pieces of cut cardboard on to a base which may be of hardboard or plywood*

[107] MARK SEVERIN *Circe and Ulysses* Engraving, printed from the wood

*This block was already split when loaned from the Golden Cockerel Press, and shows
the effect on the print of a cracked block.*

98

JAPANESE COLOUR PRINTS

APANESE colour prints deserve a section to themselves not only because their technique is one of the most highly developed but because of their influence on European painting, and on French painting in particular, during the nineteenth century. It was not by the conscious intention of some discerning connoisseur that Japanese colour prints were introduced to the painters of Paris. Oriental art had been familiar in Europe for over a century. There was a steady trade in chinoiseries; Chinese wallpapers had adorned the walls of mid-eighteenth-century mansions, and a taste for things oriental had been seen in the Royal Pavilion at Brighton.

The coloured prints which were to make such an impact on Western art were not admired even by Japanese connoisseurs, who themselves preferred 'ideal' painting. The pictures we now value were humble, 'popular' prints, and their creators were not of high social rank. So little importance was attached to these prints that they were sometimes used by the Japanese as wrapping paper. Indeed, it is said that the prints which made such a stir in Paris were discovered in the packing of some Japanese porcelain. The impact on the art world of Paris was astonishing. Artists like Degas raved about them, Van Gogh copied them, their influence was to be seen in the work of Manet; Whistler 'had the whole course of his painting diverted' by the sight of them.

To eyes brought up on 'brown realism' it was as shocking as it was delightful to find exciting and satisfying pictures made up of patches of gay colour and in which there was no attempt at chiaroscuro or modelling. Painters were inspired to explore further the aesthetic possibilities of placing masses of colour against one another, and to suggest space and depth not by light and shade (which had hitherto been thought to be indispensable) but by the subtle relationship of the shapes and their tone values. But Japanese prints revealed to European eyes (which had forgotten similar qualities in their own tradition) not only the beauties of flat pattern but also expressiveness of line of an unfamiliar kind. The quality of line achieved by the Japanese is vigorous, decorative, spontaneous and serene. It is no wonder artists were so thrilled.

The choice of subject matter, too, was congenial to European artists. The artists who designed the prints belonged to a school of painting known as the Ukiyoye, which may be translated as 'The Mirror of the Passing Show' or 'Painting of the Passing World'. The painters of the Ukiyoye took as their subject the life of the people—meaning humble people—how they worked, lived and entertained themselves. It was a kind of pictorial journalism in contrast to the 'ideal' painting where only noble and exalted subjects were considered worthy.

In Europe, too, 'ideal' classical, historical or uplifting subjects were thought to be the only subjects that merited the word 'art'. But artists were already revolting against this conception of art and Japanese colour prints suggested a way out. One sees in the work of Toulouse-Lautrec the Japanese influence in composition, in quality of line, in selection of subject matter. The influence is to be seen, not in his choice of oriental subjects but by his doing as the Japanese artist did—by looking at the life around him. James Laver said of Toulouse-Lautrec that 'he is the complete reincarnation of an Ukiyoye artist'.

Through Toulouse-Lautrec, Cheret and others, the Japanese print helped the commercial poster to become a work of art, and even today these Ukiyoye prints continue to delight and inspire further generations of artists.

But what of these prints in Japan? When and how were they made and when did they first appear? Let us answer the last question first. Prints in colour appeared in Japan in the seventeenth century and it is possible, but by no means certain, that the idea of making colour-prints from wood blocks came from Europe.* The art of so-called Chiaroscuro engraving is, in its essentials, similar to that of Japanese colour printing. Chiaroscuro prints were at their best in Europe in the work of Dürer, Hans Burkmair, and Hans Baldung Grien in the first quarter of the sixteenth century. Later in the century European missionaries landed in Tanegashima, and by the end of the century had made 150,000 converts to Christianity. There is little doubt that missionaries took with them coloured prints of saints and other religious subjects and it is suggested that the sight of these may have suggested the process to the Japanese. There is also a possibility, some would say a probability, that the Japanese learned the art from the Chinese, but they in their turn may well have derived their ideas on the subject from Europeans.

_____

*'Japanese Colour Prints', by Edward Strange, page 8 et seq.

How and when the art may have sprung up in Japan it is for scholars to establish, but it is quite certain that the prints which we admire so much were mostly issued between about 1750 and 1850, Hokusai and Utamaro being two of the greatest artists

The production of these colour prints is the result of perfect cooperation between artist, engraver (strictly 'cutter') and printer. There is no evidence that artists ever cut or printed their own designs. Prints were designed by artists who were also painters. Designing of colour-prints was regarded rather as a form of pot-boiling and Japanese writers on art at the period rarely mention this branch of an artist's work. Yet today the prints live as vital works of art, while the artist's paintings are forgotten. It may well be that there are today painters whose work as painters is of little significance, who, if they devoted their talents to print making might leave their mark in the history of the craft.

The artist drew freely with a brush held vertically, on very thin semi-transparent paper. This drawing was then handed to the engraver, who stuck

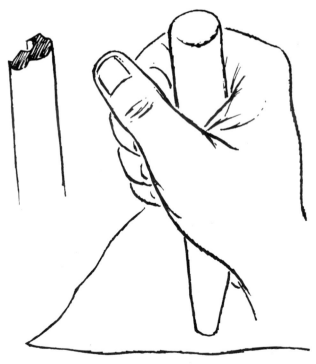

[108] *Printing a small area by means of a cut stick*

it face down (to reverse the image) onto the block. It was then oiled, or possibly scraped, so that every line of the drawing should be clearly visible. The engraver cut with a knife (held as in Fig. 26) on each side of every line and removed the background with gouges and chisels until only the drawing was left raised in bold relief.. It is evident that the original drawing was destroyed in the process and no sketches of existing prints are therefore known. But there are a number of unengraved designs extant which allow us to see how the draughtsman worked.

The block (or blocks if it was a series for a colour print) was then handed to the printer, who completed the print. The inks he used were powder colours mixed with rice paste and water and were applied with brushes. The paper was made from mulberry fibre and damped with a brush before printing. The dexterity of the printers was almost unbelievable in registering, sometimes, a large number of blocks and an even larger number of impressions. Hiroshi Yoshida, in his book 'Japanese Wood-block Printing', says that for one of his prints fourteen blocks were employed to make (believe it or not) *ninety-eight* impressions. It should be said, however, that though documentary evidence is lacking as to the maximum number of impressions ever made on one print in the late 18th and early 19th century, it is certain that the number was nowhere near the ninety-eight recorded by Hiroshi Yoshida in 1939.

[109] DERRICK HARRIS *Columbian Press* Engraving, printed from the wood

MAIN BODY OF
ILLUSTRATIONS

As we said in the Preface, most of the prints reproduced in this book have been made since the end of the second World War in 1945. Where it has been possible, through the generosity of the owners of the blocks, the original wood blocks have been used in the printing of this book and the captions state when the printing is from the wood. In some instances electros have been used.* A print from an electro is almost impossible to distinguish from a print taken direct from the wood. Because this is so, it is usual to print commercially from electros and thus preserve the original block from possible damage.

Where it was impossible (because of size or other reason) to use original blocks or electros, line blocks have been used. Generally these are not quite so satisfactory, but we believe some of the line blocks used here to be extremely good examples of the process engraver's craft. Where colour or graduations of tone make even line blocks impracticable, half-tone blocks are used.

While not omitting famous names, we have tried to show the work of younger engravers whom, we believe, deserve a wider recognition.

---

*An electro, short for electrotype, is a replica of the original woodblock. It is made by pressing wax or a special plastic onto the engraved surface of the block so that an exact embossing is made of every line. This wax or plastic is then placed in an electrolytic bath so that a shell of copper is deposited on the wax, thus forming in copper an exact replica of the printing surface of the original block. Before printing, the shell of copper just described is supported by a layer of lead and then mounted type-high.

中村の丁

[110] SHUNYEI *Shakkyo; an interpretation of the Lion dance*

風俗美人時計

酉ノ刻

屋丈

哥〜麿呂筆

泉市板

[111] UTAMARO   *The Hour of the Clock, 5–7 p.m., from Customs of*
Beautiful Women by the Clock

[112] HIROSHIGE   *The Waterfall, Koya Tama River*

[113] HIROSHIGE   *Winter, Scene on the Sumida River*

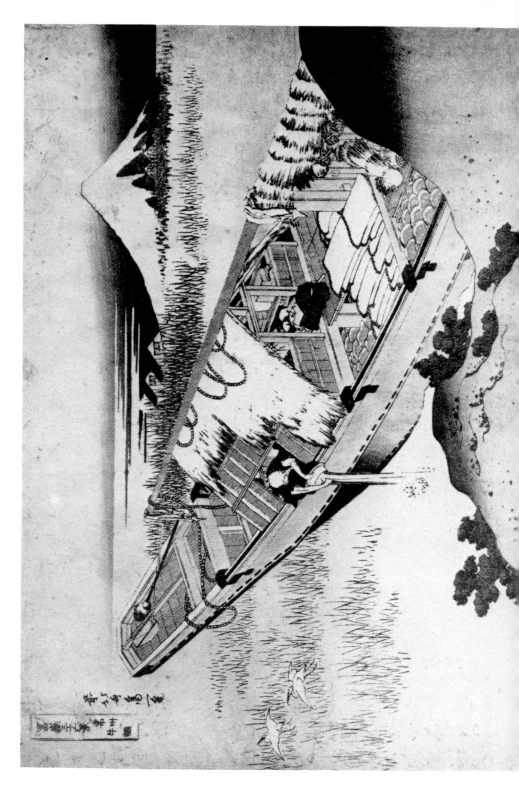

[114] HOKUSAI *Ushibori in the Province of Hitachi*

[115] PAUL GAUGUIN *Nave Nave Fenua* (*Terre delicieuse*) Cut, 13½ by 8 inches (French)

[116] EDVARD MUNCH *The Kiss* Colour woodcut, reduced (Norwegian)

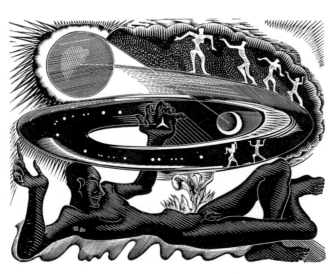

[117]
BLAIR HUGHES-STANTON
Primaeval Gods
Engraving, printed from
the wood

[118] EDVARD MUNCH *Two Beings, or the Lonely Ones* Colour woodcut, reduced
(Norwegian)

[119] ETTORE BONFATTI *Maschera Macabra* Engraving, 18⅛ by 11⅝ inches (Italian)

[120] GERTRUDE HERMES *Remote Control* Engraving, in colour, 21 by 15 inches

[121] FRANK MARTIN *Girl and Plants* Colour linocut, 16 by 11 inches

[122]   EDWARD BAWDEN   *Town Hall Yard*   Colour linocut, 24 by 16 inches

[123]   MICHAEL ROTHENSITEN   *Cockerel turning round*   Colour linocut and gesso relief
22¾ by 15⅛ inches

114

[124] JAKOB STEINHARDT *Resting Bedouins* Linocut, 18 by 15 inches (Israel)

[125] WALTER BINDER *Design on dark ground* Cut, 19½ by 14 inches (Swiss)

[126]   MICHAEL ROTHENSTEIN   *Pasture*   Linocut and stencil, 30 by 20 inches

[127]   HANS ORLOWSKI
*Sketch in ordinary writing
ink for the engraving
opposite*

128] AUGUST CERNIGOJ *Still Life* Linocut heavily printed without ink, 7¾ by 5⅝ inches (Trieste)

[129] HANS ORLOWSKI
Head of Christ
Engraving, actual size
(German)

[130] VIOTTO VIKAINEN *Summer*
Colour woodcut, 14¼ by 5½ inches
(Finnish)

[131] HANS R. BOSSHARD
Cut, 15¾ by 7¼ inches
(Swiss)

[132] HAP GRIESHABER
Composition
Cut, 58½ by 21¾ inches
(German)

[133] SEONG MOY *The Yellow Chamber* Colour woodcut, 15 by 13 inches (American)

[134] M. DOMJAN *Thistles* Colour cut, 18½ by 13¼ inches (Hungarian)

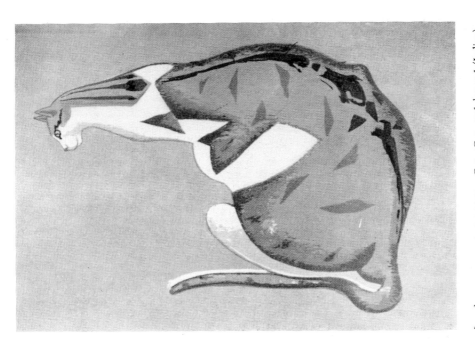

[139] OSCAR DALVIT *Abstract* Cut, 16 by 11¼ inches (Swiss)

[138] ALEKSANDER SIVERT *Staircase* Colour woodcut, 8¼ by 5⅝ inches (Jugoslav)

[141] ADJA JUNKERS *Dead Bird* Colour woodcut, 17 by 19¼ inches (American)

[140] ANTONIO FRASCONI *The Storm is Coming* Colour woodcut, 22 by 15½ inches (American)

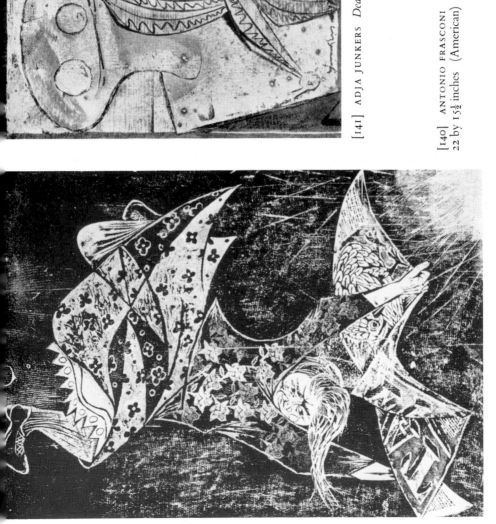

[142]   EMIL ZBINDEN   *Staumauerbau*   Cut, 10½ by 7¾ inches (Swiss)

[143]   F. TIDEMAND-JOHANNESSEN   *May Trees in Rain*   Cut, 22¾ by 17½ inches
(Norwegian)

[144]   RUPERT SHEPHARD   Colour linocut

[145]   WALTER BATTISS   *Mothers and Children near waterfall*   Cut, 16½ by 11¾ inches
(South African)

[146] PIETRO SANCHINI *La Gabbia* Engraving, 17¾ by 17¼ inches (Italian)

[147] DAVID JONES *Illustration from The Deluge* Engraving, printed from the wood

[148] JOHN BUCKLAND-WRIGHT *Endymion* Engraving, printed from the wood

[149] RODERIC BARRETT
Bike ride Engraving
Printed from the wood

[150] BLAIR HUGHES-STANTON
Vignette Engraving
printed from the wood

[151] CECIL KEELING *Zastrozzi* Engraving, printed from the wood

[152]   LUTHER ROBERTS   *Illustration*   Engraving, printed from the wood

[153] PETER BARKER-MILL From *A Voyage Round the World* Engraving, from the wood

[154] PETER BARKER-MILL
From *A Voyage Round the World*
Engraving, from the wood

[155] DAVID GENTLEMAN
Scott of the Antarctic
Engraving, actual size

134

[156]   GEOFFREY WALES   From *Nelson's Letters*   Engraving, from the wood

[157]   DAVID GENTLEMAN   *The Waggoners*   Engraving, actual size

[158] JOHN R. BIGGS From Spencer's *Epithalamium* Engraving, from the wood

[159] JOHN R. BIGGS From Spencer's *Epithalamium* Engraving, from the wood

[160] JOHN R. BIGGS *Fishing at Rickmansworth* Engraving, from the wood

[161] DERRICK HARRIS *Joseph Andrews* Engraving, from the wood

[162] DERRICK HARRIS *Joseph Andrews* Engraving, from the wood

138

[163] ERIC RAVILIOUS *Twelfth Night* Engraving, printed from the wood

[164] EUGENE MECIKALSKI *A Heron in the Four Phases of the Moon*
Engraving (American), 8 by 6 inches

[165] PAUL NASH *Abd-er-Rhaman in Paradise* Engraving, actual size

[166]   V. LE CAMPION   *Manon Lescaut*   Engraving, actual size (French)

[167]
MARK SEVERIN
Circe and Ulysses
Engraving
from the wood

[168]   V. LE CAMPION
Manon Lescaut
Engraving,
actual size
(French)

[169] JOAN HASSALL
Pride & Prejudice
Engraving
actual size

[170]
DAVID GENTLEMAN
Vignette Engraving
actual size

[172]
JOHN O'CONNOR
We Happy Few
Engraving
from the wood

[173] TRANQUILLO MARANGONI *The Artist's Family* Engraving, 15 by 9¾ inches (Italian)

[174] LEONARD BASKIN
Blake—Death Mask
Engraving, actual size
(American)

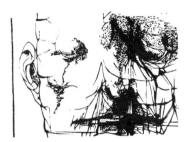

[175] LEONARD BASKIN
Blake—a fragment Engraving
actual size (American)

[176] LEONARD BASKIN
Blake—Death Mask
Engraving, actual size
(American)

[177]   BRUNO BOBAK   *Rock Hill*   Engraving, 8⅛ by 5⅛ inches (Canadian)

[178]   ROCKWELL KENT   *Big Baby*   Engraving, 6 by 4½ inches (American)

147

[179]   ALISTAIR BELL   *Boats at Newlyn*   Engraving, actual size (Canadian)

[18·2] WILLI THALER
Christ at Emmaus
Cut, 6¾ by 4¼ inches
(Swiss)

[183]
THIJS MAUVE
Ex Libris
Engraving
actual size
(Dutch)

[184] BERT BOUMAN *Head of Christ* Cut, reduced

[185] J. J. DE GRAVE *La fille* Cut (Belgian)

[186] MARJAN TRSAR   *The Circus Family*   Cut, 15¾ by 11⅝ inches (Jugoslav)

153

[187] MAKSIM SEDEJ *Interior* Cut, 11 by 7¾ inches (Jugoslav)

[188] SLAVI SOUCEK *Composition* Linocut, 20¼ by 13¼ inches (Austrian)

154

[189] TOON WEGNER *Chess Players* Cut, 15 by 10½ inches (Dutch)

[190] RIKO DEBENJAK *Women of Istria* Engraving, 12 by 8½ inches (Jugoslav)

[191]
HANS ORLOWSKI
Orpheus
Engraving, actual size
(German)

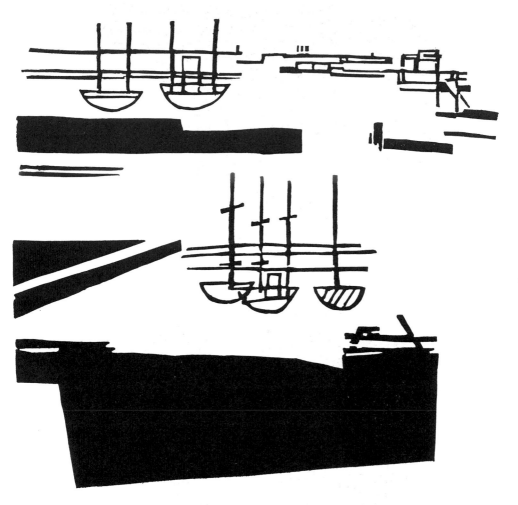

[192]   GUSTAV K. BECK   *Shipping in Harbour*   Cut, 13 by 12½ inches (Austrian)

[193]
J. B. SLEPER
Ex Libris
Engraving, actual size
(Dutch)

[194] TONE KRALJ *Harvest* Engraving, 14¾ by 11⅛ inches (Jugoslav)

[195] VASSIL ZAKHARIEV *Raspberry Pickers* Cut, 19½ by 16¾ inches (Bulgarian)

[196] PAM REUTER
Book-plate Engraving
actual size (Dutch)

[197] LEONA PIERCE
Boy on Rope Cut
actual size (American)

[198] FRANS MASEREEL *Interior* Engraving, reduced (French)

[199] LUIS GUALAZZI
The Procession
Engraving, 9½ by 7 inches
(Italian)

[200] BUDAGOSSKI
Portrait of a Poet
Engraving, actual size
(Russian)

[201] BOZIDAR JAKAC *Gargoyles and Notre Dame* Cut, 15½ by 12¾ inches (Jugoslav)

[202] PIKOV *Portrait of the actress Babanova.* Engraving, actual size (Russian)

[203] PETER PENDREY *The Artamonovs* Cut, actual size

[204] WANG YEN *Funeral* Chinese

[205] FOLK ARTIST *Household work* Chinese

BIBLIOGRAPHY

TECHNICAL

WOOD ENGRAVING, R. John Beedham, *Faber & Faber, London*, 1938. A short, sound introduction to the craft of wood engraving by one of the best reproductive engravers of his day.

WOOD-ENGRAVING, *A manual of instruction*, W. J. Linton, *George Bell & Sons, London*, 1884. A book intended to instruct the more sensitive type of 19th century trade engraver, but its technical advice is of value to artists now.

A TREATISE ON WOOD ENGRAVING — *Historical and Practical*. W. A. Chatto and John Jackson, *Chatto & Windus, London*, 1838. A historical survey of woodcutting and wood engraving from the earliest times until the early nineteenth century, together with, perhaps, the a most thorough account of the technique of wood engraving known to us.

WOOD ENGRAVING, George E. Mackley, *The National Magazine Co, London*, 1948. A readable and reliable instructional book by an accomplished engraver. Numerous illustrations and diagrams engraved by the author and a few others.

YOUR WOOD-ENGRAVING, Mark F. Severin, *Sylvan Press, London*, 1953. A small book of instruction in the craft of engraving by the distinguished Belgian artist and illustrated with 16 of his engraved diagrams.

WOOD-ENGRAVING, Iain Macnab, *Pitman, London*, 1947. A short, rather chatty introduction to the art and craft with half-tone reproductions of engravings by various artists.

ENGRAVING ON WOOD, John Farleigh, *Dryad Press, Leicester*, 1954. This is a brief, easy-to-follow book of instruction with illustrations, mostly by the author.

GRAVEN IMAGE, *An autobiographical text book*, John Farleigh, *Macmillan*, 1940. Many illustrations by the author and some by Bernard Shaw.

WOOD ENGRAVING & WOODCUTS, Clare Leighton, *The Studio*, 1932. A sound introduction to the craft with photographs of the hands of artists at work, diagrams and some engravings.

WOODCUTS, *or The Practice of engraving and cutting upon wood*, D. P. Bliss, *Dryad Handicrafts*. Sixteen pages only, but as sound as it is entertaining; primarily about engraving.

WOOD-BLOCK PRINTING, F. Morley Fletcher, *Pitman, London*, 1916. The sub-title is 'A description of the craft of woodcutting and colour printing based on the Japanese practice'. It is perhaps the best of the very few technical manuals on the craft of wood-*cutting* available in English. With diagrams, photographs and reproductions of prints.

JAPANESE WOOD-BLOCK PRINTING, Hiroshi Yoshida, *Sanseido Co., Tokyo*, 1939. A detailed account by an expert Japanese practitioner of the craft as still practised in Japan. With diagrams, photographs and 'pro-pressives' of an actual hand-burnished print.

TOOLS & MATERIALS ILLUSTRATING THE JAPANESE METHOD OF COLOUR PRINTING, Edward Strange, *V. & A. Museum, London*, 1924. This useful pamphlet is a descriptive catalogue of a collection in the Museum.

JAPANESE WOOD-CUTTING & WOODCUT PRINTING, T. Tokuno, *U.S.A. National Museum, Washington*, 1893.

WOODCUTS AND SOME WORDS, Gordon Craig, *J. M. Dent, London*, 1924. Autobiography and instruction in a lively and personal English style, giving as much information and inspiration about the art of the theatre as about engraving. A great joy!

WOODCUTS AND WOOD ENGRAVINGS, Noel Rooke, *Print Collectors Club, London*, 1926. The subtitle is 'Being a lecture . . . on the origin and character of the present school of engraving and cutting'. The engraved diagrams are a model of their kind.

THE ART OF WOOD ENGRAVING, A Practical Handbook, Gilks, 1866.

HOW I MAKE WOODCUTS & WOOD ENGRAVINGS, Hans Alexander Mueller, *American Artists Group Inc., New York*, 1945. A personal approach to the art and craft by an expert American practitioner, illustrated entirely by his own work.

ILLUSTRATION & REPRODUCTION, John R. Biggs, *Blandford Press, London*, 1950.

THE ART OF WOOD ENGRAVING, Francis M. Reynolds, *B. E. Hale, New York*, 1879. 39pp. Illustrated.

THE TECHNIQUE OF THE COLOR WOOD-CUT, Walter Joseph Phillips, *Brown-Robertson Co., New York*, 1926. 63pp. Illustrated

BLOCK PRINTING CRAFT, Raymond W. Perry, *The Manual Arts Press*, 1938. *Peoria, Illinois.* (Books on the Arts.) 143pp. Illustrated

A MANUAL OF INSTRUCTION IN THE ART OF WOOD ENGRAVING, S. E. Fuller, *Joseph Watson, Boston*, 1867. With illustrations by the author.

BLOCK PRINTING, John R. Bacon, *J. R. Bacon, New York*, 1924 (?). 4 pages of text. Illustrated.

HISTORICAL AND CRITICAL

A HISTORY OF WOOD-ENGRAVING, Douglas Percy Bliss, *J. M. Dent & Sons, London*, 1928. A readably, indeed racily, written history of engraving by an artist of imagination. The many illustrations are selected with a feeling for scholarship and with a sense of humour.

WOODCUT/WOOD ENGRAVING, Imre Reiner, *Public Publishing Co., London*, 1947. Twelve pages of text and about a hundred illustrations of prints from A.D. 868 to 1945.

A BRIEF HISTORY OF WOOD-ENGRAVING, Joseph Cundall, *Sampson Low, Marston & Co., London*, 1895. Good as far as it goes.

THE WOODCUT, an annual, edited by Herbert Furst, *The Fleuron Ltd., London. No.* I, 1927; *No.* II, 1928; *No.* III, 1929; *No.* IV, 1930. Scholarly articles and an excellent selection of engravings of the 20's.

WOOD ENGRAVING OF THE 1930's, Clare Leighton, *The Studio, London*, 1936. An interesting collection of engravings of that period from many countries.

THE MODERN WOODCUT, Herbert Furst, *John Lane, The Bodley Head, London*, 1924. About a third of the book is historical, one chapter is an account of the craft by N. Thomas Smith, and the remainder is critical comment and reproductions (about 200) of twentieth-century woodcuts, woodengravings and linocuts.

THE DREAM OF POLIPHILUS, *Department of Science & Art, South Kensington*, 1893. Facsimile reproductions of 168 woodcuts from the famous 'Hypnerotomachia Poliphili' (Venice, 1499).

ENGLISH WOODENGRAVING, 1900–1950, Thomas Balston, *Art & Technics*, *London*, 1951. An urbane essay and an excellent selection of engravings in the orthodox manner.

MEMOIR OF THOMAS BEWICK, Thomas Bewick, *John Lane, The Bodley Head, London*, 1924. This is a classic of its kind. It is the autobiography of the great naturalist and wood engraver in which we see the man behind the engravings and something of the society behind the man. Worth reading as literature and for the information about the art and craft of wood-engraving.

THOMAS BEWICK & HIS PUPILS, Austin Dobson, *Chatto & Windus, London*, 1889. A well-written and scholarly account that is as readable as it is informative.

WOOD ENGRAVINGS BY THOMAS BEWICK, John Rayner, *Penguin Books Ltd., London*, 1947. An easy-to-read introduction to a selection of Bewick's engravings as representative as the size of the book allows.

THOMAS BEWICK: A RÉSUMÉ OF HIS WORK, Graham Reynolds, *Art & Technics, London*, 1949.

LIFE & WORKS OF THOMAS BEWICK, David Croal Thomson, *Art Journal Office, London*, 1882.

THOMAS BEWICK, Montague Weekley, *Oxford University Press, Oxford*, 1953.

WOOD ENGRAVING SINCE 1890, *Pitman, London*, 1932. A technical and critical book on the craft by a practitioner.

THE FOLLOWERS OF WILLIAM BLAKE, Laurence Binyon, *Halton & Truscott Smith, London*, 1925. A sensitive and discerning essay, as one would expect from a poet; with reproductions of all the wood engravings by Calvert.

BLAKE'S ILLUSTRATIONS FOR THORNTON'S VIRGIL, Geoffrey Keynes, *The Nonesuch Press, London*, 1937. A scholarly essay and reproductions (the best yet) of Blake's engravings for Thornton's Virgil.

HISTORY OF WOODCUT, Arthur M. Hind, *Constable & Co., London*, 1935. A model of scholarship. Two large volumes dealing with cuts of the 15th century; copiously illustrated.

THE HISTORY OF WOOD ENGRAVING IN AMERICA, W. J. Linton, *George Bell & Sons, London*, 1882. Deals with reproductive engraving.

THE NEW WOODCUT, Malcolm Salaman, *The Studio, London*, 1930. An international selection of engravings with commentary.

JAPANESE COLOUR PRINTS, Edward F. Strange, *V. & A. Museum, London*, 1931. This admirable volume contains a chapter on the technique, a history and commentary and over 80 plates.

CATALOGUE OF EARLY GERMAN & FLEMISH WOODCUTS, Campbell Dodgson, *British Museum*, 1903–11.

WOODCUTS OF DÜRER, Edited by T. D. Barlow, *Penguin Books, London*, 1948.

THE CHIAROSCURISTS OF THE XVI–XVIII CENTURIES, Anton Reichel, *W. Heffer, Cambridge*. A fine selection of colour prints. The reproductions are unusually faithful. Short text.

HISTORY OF THE CATNACH PRESS, Chalres Hindley, *London*, 1886. An entertaining account of the publisher of cheap books, broadsheets, etc. Many reproductions.

BANBURY CHAP BOOKS AND NURSERY TOY BOOK LITERATURE, Edwin Pearson, *A. Reader, London*, 1890. An essay illustrated by several hundred original woodcut blocks.

MODERN WOODCUTTERS, a series of four booklets containing prints by (1) Gwen Raverat, (2) Frank Brangwyn, (3) Sturge Moore, (4) Edward Wadsworth.

DEUTSCHE HOLZSCHNITTE DES XX JAHRHUNDERTS, IM INSEL VERLAG, Wiesbaden, 1955.

HIRTENLEBEN 36 HOLZSHNITTE (woodcuts), Aristide Maillol, Insel Verlag, Wiesbaden, 1955.

CHINESISCHE HOLZSCHNITTE, Insel Verlag, Weisbaden, 1954. Coloured reproductions.

FRANZÖSISCHE GRAPHIC DES XX JAHRHUNDERTS, Buchheim Verlag, Feldafing, 1956.

EDVARD MUNCH, Buchheim Verlag, Feldafing, 1954.

JAPANESE COLOUR PRINTS, Arthur W. Ruffy, *V. & A. Museum, London*, 1952. Being a quarto volume the illustrations are larger and rather better than in the other books on Japanese prints mentioned above. The Introduction is most informative and well written.

ENGRAVINGS ON WOOD, by members of the Society of American Wood Engravers, with an introduction and descriptive text by W. M. Laffan, Society of American Wood Engravers, *Harper & Bros., New York*, 1887. 25 pl.

WOOD ENGRAVING AND WOOD ENGRAVERS, Hiram Campbell Merrill, *Society of Printers of Boston, Boston,* 1937. 15pp. frontispiece. 500 copies printed.

A WOODCUT MANUAL, Julius J. Lankes, *Henry Holt & Co, New York,* 1932. 122pp. Illustrated.

THE ART OF THE AMERICAN WOOD ENGRAVER, Philip Gilbert Hamerton, *C. Scribner's Sons, New York,* 1894. 2 v. (Limited edition of 100 copies. 40 India proofs to accompany the text.) Catalogue with biographical notes and a bibliography.

AMERICAN WOODCUTS AND ENGRAVINGS, 1670–1800, by Lawrence C. Wroth and Marion W. Adams; with an introduction by Clarence S. Brigham. *The Associates of the John Carter Brown Library, Providence,* 1944. 44pp. Illustrated. (Printed at the Southworth-Anthoensen Press, Portland, Maine.)

AMERICAN WOODCUTS, 1670–1950; a survey of woodcuts and wood engravings in the United States by Una E. Johnson, *Brooklyn Museum, Brooklyn, New York,* 1950. Catalogue of an exhibition. Bibliography.

ACKNOWLEDGMENTS

EVERY AUTHOR owes much to others not only for information or facilities for study freely given but for counsel and encouragement. Among those who have helped in this way is Frank Martin, A.R.E., the secretary of the Society of Wood Engravers, who also lent books, prints, and addresses of artists, read the proofs and specially cut the block on page 13.

As the collection of prints for the book involved correspondence in many languages which I do not understand, I am particularly grateful to my colleague Raymond Cowern, A.R.A., who was always ready at a moment's notice to translate letters in German, French, or Italian. Thanks are also due to J. J. Meyer for some German translations, to R. Jinks and Luther Roberts for reading the manuscript, and to the latter for the engraving on page 13.

I am grateful to all artists who have lent their work for reproduction, particularly those who have lent the original blocks. Special thanks are due to Mr. Christopher Sandford, of the Golden Cockerel Press, for the loan of the blocks for plates number 104, 107, 117, 147, 148, 150, 151, 153, 154, 156, 163, 165, 167, 172, 206; to Mr. Charles Ede, of the Folio Society, for plates number 1, 6, 105, 161, 162, 166, 168, 169, 171, 203.

Among many others I must thank are Lynd Ward, President of the Society of American Graphic Artists; Dr. Rumpel, Secretary of XYLON, Secretary of the Société Internationale des Graveurs sur Bois; Emil Zbinden, Prof. Hans Orlowski, Tranquillo Maragoni, Kathleen Fenwick of the National Gallery of Canada (for plates number 177, 179, 180), Karl Kup of the New York Public Library. The Victoria & Albert Museum (for plates number 110, 111, 112, 113, 114) and the Arts Council (for plates number 115, 116, 118).

INDEX
Including Index of Artists

Bold figures indicate page number of illustrations

174

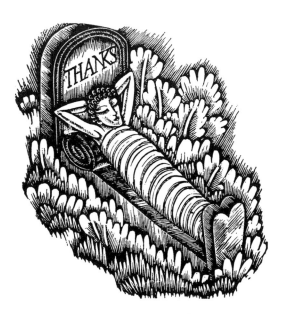

[206] ERIC GILL *Tail piece* Engraving